Ban'ya Natsuishi's

World of Dreams: An Intensive Study of Selected Haiku

夏石番矢の夢幻世界　その俳句の集中研究

Edited by

Santosh Kumar

ISBN: 978-93-85945-80-9
First Edition: 2017

$15 / £12 / Rs. 400

Cyberwit.net
HIG 45 Kaushambi Kunj, Kalindipuram
Allahabad - 211011 (U.P.) India
http://www.cyberwit.net
Tel: +(91) 9415091004 +(91) (532) 2552257
E-mail: info@cyberwit.net

Printed at Repro India Limited.

Preface

It is quite important to understand the meaning of haiku, an unrhymed Japanese poetic form. Haiku consists of of 17 syllables arranged in three lines of 5, 7, and 5 syllables respectively. This critical book reveals a thoroughly apt and profound analysis of Ban'ya's haiku poetry by eminent authors across the globe. No doubt, the book presents highly significant and valuable criticism of Ban'ya as one of the greatest contemporary haiku poets.

Let us ponder on what makes a good poem. A good poem is 'a reaching-out toward expression; an effort to find fulfillment. A complete poem is one where the emotion has found its thought and the thought has found the words' (Robert Frost). Dylan Thomas aptly remarks: "A good poem is a contribution to reality. The world is never the same once a good poem has been added to it. A good poem helps to change the shape of the universe, helps to extend everyone's knowledge of himself and the world around him". All the elements that constitute a good poem as revealed in these critical observations are fully visible in Ban'ya's numberless poems.

I trust that all readers will have deeper understanding of Ban'ya's haiku world after reading this book providing critical perspectives full of profound insight into his artless art of writing haiku. All the critical essays included in this book offer highly impressive and deep analysis on the most significant features of Ban'ya's immortal haiku which never fail to create 'a sudden moment of stillness or realization'.

The critical articles selected and included in this book aptly examine what are the most innovative features of Ban'ya's haiku poetry, and what were his means to write his haiku. Several critics have estimated the merits of great haiku of Ban'ya by examining and analyzing line with line. I trust that this would be of immense help to enjoy and comprehend his haiku world.

After reading this critical book, we are sure to come to the conclusion that Ban'ya in his haiku very aptly blends pleasure with truth. Ban'ya's keen observation helps him to deliver universal truths through his haiku which always delight the readers, because they are full of attractive images and strong impressions.

The book brings together critical evaluation and responses representing a wide range of authors from different parts of the world. The learned contributors are Adam Donaldson Powell, Aiswarya T Anish, Amitabh Mitra, Anna Cates, Kalyan Panja, Malini, Marta Knobloch, Santosh Kumar, Sayumi Kamakura, Shirley Bolstok and Usha Kishore. I am quite obliged and thankful to them for their high-quality scholarly critical articles.

I hope the comprehensive critical book penetrating into a new level of literary criticism of Ban'y's haiku poetry will be quite useful for students interested in haiku poetry, scholars, teachers, libraries and researchers.

- Santosh Kumar

Contents

An endless helix
Sings silently
Inside our body

A Modern Master of Haiku Paints The Collective Conscience

Adam Donaldson Powell

A gong sounds somewhere in the distance, and in the silence that ensues the reverberations of the collective conscience precipitate a collage of impressions that are at once familiar, and yet far beyond the accepted structures of perception. In this impressive collection of contemporary haiku, Ban'ya Natsuishi expertly challenges and coaxes the reader to join him in a flight of fancy – in and out of reality and illusion – not so unlike the great surrealist Salvador Dali. Both the reader and the flying pope take to the air, suspended above the Earth like an out-of-body experience ... observing from afar, and yet experiencing the dream-like state as if it were totally real – as a sort of déjà vu recollection of the fringes between zazen and newspaper headlines ... or perhaps the CNN rolling news texts, floating across the bottom of the television screen. While it may be tempting to point out Natsuishi as *l'Enfant terrible* of contemporary haiku writing, his impudence is not intended to shock. It is, in fact, this sense of detachment in the author that binds together the childlike, the serious, the sarcastic, the humorous and the reflective – resulting in a splattering of surrealistic images that pose far more questions to the reader than give blatant commentary. Because of the masterly free flying construction, the reader is just as easily won over to the haiku of Ban'ya Natsuishi as he/she might be to adventuresome comic books and animated films.

True enough, there is much observation embedded in these pearls of writing: sparkling semi-precious jewels singing, dancing, and jabbering now and then about such themes as politics, haiku writing without seasonal references, the loneliness of papal responsibility, and the burden of conscience. However, the real artistry of this work is perhaps the succession of painterly haiku frescoes, all variations on the same theme: the illusion of consciousness.

Do read this book several times – forward and backwards, and even starting in the middle and proceeding in any direction ... sometimes dancing back and forth. There are many hidden levels within the poems, the silent connections in between the poems and in the work as a whole.

-Adam Donaldson Powell, Oslo, 2008 (based upon the English version of "Flying Pope"). "Flying Pope" is published by cyberwit.net.

Essay About the Haiku of Ban'ya Natsuishi Contemporary Haiku: the renaissance and the transformation.

Adam Donaldson Powell

Literary criticism (2008) by Adam Donaldson Powell (based upon "Right Eye in Twilight", published by Wasteland Press, USA, 2006, ISBN13: 978-1-60047-016-5 and ISBN10: 1-60047-016-5, 62 pages, paperback, US\$12; and "Earth Pilgrimage" (Pellegrinaggio terrestre), published by Albalibri Editore, Italy, 2007, ISBN 88-89618-52-3 and ISBN 978-88-89618-52-3, 146 pages, paperback, •10).

As I sit before the screen of my laptop computer, the fat of my palms resting on the flat area of the keyboard and my fingers poised to attack – I close my eyes and begin to breathe rhythmically, as a concert pianist. I feel certain of the notes that are about to flow through the tentacles of my body-mind-spirit machine, but immediately become encapsulated by the poetry of my own breathing. And in the cello-like dark mellow tones, underscoring the inevitability of one breath following another, I am at one with the driving impulse behind the art of Ban'ya Natsuishi. That impulse, that drive has many names but is perhaps best described as "satori" (meaning a state of spiritual enlightenment ... but also quite simply 'insight').

The haiku of Natsuishi have many dimensions, and forms of expression. Perhaps the most common factors are the renaissance and transformation of duality, and the exposure of illusion caused by the folly of spiritual separation. Natsuishi has the uncanny talent of presenting perspectives from all angles – and yet, never contradictory in spite of individual or collective social experience. True insight, and effective artistic communication, is never exclusive or preaching ... but rather expanding and questioning. It is exemplified by the ability to combine perspectives of the 'external looking inward' and the 'internal looking outward', the left side of the brain in tandem with the right side, the virtuosity of a well-trained and natural violinist on an equal footing with the exquisitely understated harmonies of a monk choir.

And still, Natsuishi does not cheat us of a glimpse into his own humanity – in fact, in "Right Eye in Twilight" he takes us along on his own personal journey, which both literally and poetically describes a search for vision ('insight'). Here, the author invites the reader to accompany him in his rapturous process – ascending toward a state of satori that had nevertheless always existed in each of us from the very first times we opened (and closed) our eyes. It is this nakedness that reveals the childishness in us all – the fear, the frustration, the wantonness, the infatuation with the process itself – and that creates sublime poetry, in balance with our adult, intellectual and rational expression.

From "Right Eye in Twilight":

A black horse
slowly getting white
in the wood

and

New York –
the terror of dust
toying with sundown

and

Water is a white nebula
within me
blown by winds

and the very beautiful

On a morning swamp
I see
the Palace of Versailles

For me, the very essence of the 'satori' of Ban'ya Natsuishi is exemplified in the most delicate and sensitive haiku found in the collection entitled "Earth Pilgrimage" (Pellegrinaggio terrestre). Each of these multi-faceted diamonds express both intimacy with oneself, one's surroundings and with Spirit – free from separation. And yet they do not seek to deny the harshness of living on Terra, but rather allow the reader to see the effects of turning the face of the diamond – just slightly enough to get lost in the momentary light capturing us, our blindness giving true vision for an instant.

A few priceless examples follow:

Shoved off the stairs –
falling I become
a rainbow

and

From the reed marsh
New York appears
like an old UFO

and

A new moon –
the sublimity of the orchid
not yet achieved

and

An almond in bloom
leaning against
cactuses

and finally

Even in the clouds
a mute and a deaf person
arguing with each other

Contemporary haiku art simply does not get any better than as expressed in "Earth Pilgrimage". It is both a renaissance and a transformation – of the essence, and the ever expanding and contracting nature of the haiku.

And my breathing continues in empathetic harmony, at one with the insight and vision of Ban'ya Natsuishi.

- Adam Donaldson Powell, Oslo, 2008

Expression of Emotions in the International / Multilingual Haiku of Ban'ya Natsuishi

Adam Donaldson Powell

Some old-fashioned "experts" still insist that human emotions in haiku are only to be expressed in figurative ways through depictions of nature, while others are venturing into somewhat more obvious analogies. I - myself - am a bit wary of the pitfalls of falling prey to reading too much into the subtleties of haiku, or to limit the usage of such expressions of subtlety to Japanese culture and tradition.

There are many opinions circulating regarding the mechanics and functions of haiku-writing, as well as some individuals who would seem to maintain that the only good haiku-writers are those who follow strict Japanese tradition. As I have written elsewhere, contemporary haiku - and perhaps especially international haiku and haiku adaptations into other languages - must address many cultural and linguistic differences that may challenge traditional Japanese rules regarding classical haiku, including but not limited to meter, linguistic and culturally-associated rhythms and sounds of words employed, expansion of time beyond "the moment" etc.

I was impressed to read the following in Natsuishi's essay entitled "Composing Haiku in a Foreign Country" (A Future Waterfall, 2004, Red Moon Press, ISBN 1-893959-46-5, USA):

"[Nevertheless,] not many Japanese Haiku poets have been open to foreign experiences ... The main reason is their idée fixe about nature ... This situation has effectively prevented Japanese haiku poets from looking at a foreign land from a non-Japanese perspective. Foreign landscapes remain largely alien and incomprehensible.

"A haiku poet in a foreign country has many occasions for inspiration. Many things provoke him to look at them from new and different angles — provide him with a new insight and a different sensibility. This is the way it should be. After all, one principal purpose of haiku is to discover something new in everything and to reveal it to the world ...

"More than three hundred years after Bashô, I am trying to create in my haiku diverse, astonishing traditions and phenomena of the whole world."

It occurs to me that the cultural associative expertise required in international haiku and haiku in translation is perhaps especially significant in regards to communication of emotion - both viscerally and figuratively. While classical Japanese haiku expresses emotions more figuratively than directly, modern forms of haiku and international / non-Japanese haiku forms would appear to be experimenting with and stretching the "old and the traditional" into more "liberal" expressions of emotion and usages of *kigo*.

Ban'ya Natsuishi is classically-schooled and does employ many traditional Japanese forms in his haiku-writing, but he is also constantly exploring the haiku in literary evolution. His work with World Haiku presents special challenges and many new possibilities in regards to the internationalization of contemporary haiku-writing.

Some outstanding examples of innovative contemporary haiku by Natsuishi follow:

from "A Future Waterfall", 2004, Red Moon Press, ISBN 1-893959-46-5, USA:

page 13:

From the future
a wind arrives
that blows the waterfall apart

page 18:

Cherry blossoms fall:
newspapers
suck in a great deal of blood

In Tokyo
the angry flower is
a snow crystal

page 23

Into the Sea of Japan
lightning's tail
is plunged

page 31

On my tongue
a temple appears
allegro

page 43

Above the sea
lightning violates
the Galaxy

Tunisian
blue lightens
the swindling

and from "Endless Helix", 2007, Cyberwit.net, ISBN 978-81-8253-072-0, India:

Perfection
is the symphony of the valley —
a stray sheep

Parfaite est la symphonie
de la vallée —
un mouton perdu

Sinfonía perfecta
en el valle
la oveja perdida

A cloud beyond any shape —
we have lost
our memory

Un nuage au-delà de toute forme —
nous avons perdu
notre mémoire

Una nube que tiene
más que todas las formas ...
¿ perdimos nuestra memoria?

The sea of tears
always waiting
for our haiku

La mer de larmes
attend toujours
notre haiku

El mar de lágrimas
siempre espera por
nuestro haiku

page 53

Under the scorching sun
I have forgotten
how to love myself

Sous le soleil brûlant
j'ai oublié
comment je pourrais m'aimer

Bajo el abrasante sol
he olvidado
como amarme a mí mismo

Page 87, Dream no. 10

One after another our soldiers bleed to death.
We have lost any reason to press ahead.
We make up the blood pressure readings of our king,
the balance so to speak, of his rivers underneath.
Yet, we raise lances, dash forward,
And my voice is drowned out trying to hold us back.

Page Dream No. 12

Scratched.
Beaten.
Cut.
Ice sheds tears.
A beauty dances over this frozen swell.
She falls down by its caprice.

It is my premise that expression of emotions in art is not merely a question of perspective of nature, but concerns color, form, verb form, sound, meter and time as well.

In the above examples Natsuishi plays with the "rules" most creatively, experimenting with time ("a *future* waterfall"), direct and less direct references to emotions, sometimes more liberal approaches to the usage of kigo, and purposeful liberation from 5-7-5 meter in favor of culturally-effective adaptations in English, Spanish and French (I cannot comment on other languages which I do not understand). Successful adaptation of haiku from Japanese (or another language) to other languages is not merely a question of cultural and linguisitic translation but perhaps also entails a oneness in expression in the original language that at times surpasses literary and cultural norms in the mother tongue in order to achieve a more universal expression.

The ability to successfully make creative decisions depends on the artist's understanding of tradition (where artistic expression norms have hailed from) as well as the understanding of how to employ intentional techniques to achieve desired new forms of expression. Decisions regarding usage of meter, form, sound, suggestion, time, length etc. should be conscious and intentional, and yet give the appearance of evenness and technical ease and dexterity. A technically or emotionally difficult passage in a work of music, literature or art should appear as effortless in execution as a technically or emotionally easy one. Here

Ban'ya Natsuishi unabashedly shows his mastery of artistic execution and suggestiveness and his intelligence in decisionmaking and planning — resulting in a natural feeling recognizable by readers from various cultures, traditions and in many languages.

Despite his intellectual and technical expertise, Natsuishi has loftier goals than merely to find new ways of expressing emotions. He says himself: "My concern is not expressing emotion in a new way, but something deeper than emotion is my target."

- Adam Donaldson Powell, Oslo, 2009.

Short Essay on Presentation of World Haiku

Adam Donaldson Powell

An essay based upon the following multilingual haiku books by Ban'ya Natsuishi:

MADARAK / BIRDS, 50 HAIKU, including aquarelles by Éva Pápai, translations by Ban'ya Natsuishi, Jack Galmitz and Judit Vihar, published in 2007, Balassi Kiadó, Budapest, Hungary, ISBN 978-963-506-743-5; and *VOICES FROM THE CLOUDS,* translations by Leons Briedis, Ban'ya Natsuishi, Jim Kacian and James Shea, published in 2008, Minerva, Latvia, ISBN 978-9984-637-42-5.

World haiku books are generally characterized by bilingualism or multilingualism, i.e. haiku books published with translations or adaptations in one or more languages in addition to the mother tongue of the haiku writer. This is also true of the world haiku books of Ban'ya Natsuishi. Mr. Natuishi's literary adeptness is well-established - both by fans and reviewers such as myself, and by the international and Japanese literary communities at large. What I would like to address in this essay is presentation — the function of haiku with translations / adaptations in the same book, and the function of haiku together with and in competition with art / photography. In other words: the aesthetic dimensions and considerations.

I have previously commented upon the now-popular combination of haiku with photography: "I have written elsewhere that I prefer photography books without captions and titles ... this is often a sensitive and over-debated question. However, I do not believe that it is solely a question of aesthetics or subjective 'likes and dislikes' / personal preferences. There are also the questions of functionality, total artistic impression as well as technical questions such as 'when is more actually too much?' Are the haiku captions or poetry? Do they serve a complementary function or an interpretative function, and are they (in fact) essential to understanding the photographs? Is the placement of these haiku optimal, or would another approach to combining photography and haiku have a stronger effect? These are all questions that strike me in my own personal experience ..." It is important to me as reader and reviewer that presentation of haiku in book form satisfies the underlying aesthetic values of simplicity, space for thought and reflection, and maximal visual interpretation by the reader himself / herself. Furthermore, it is important to me that the haiku and the artwork function both on their own as artistic expressions AND together as complements, but not as explanations or rationalizations of each other. They should not be in competition with one another, and not too interpretative of each other.

This applies as well to presentation of haiku translations and adaptations alongside one another. The number and placement of haiku in translation / adaptation must not create a sense of constriction in regards to space, or be too overwhelming in terms of text. There are many possible solutions to these challenges, including: separating haiku and photography / art into different sections in the book, limiting the number of translations / adaptations, utilizing artistic imagery that is less concrete (eg. abstract imagery, painted calligraphy which gives a simple visual presentation, etc.) or watercolors or another medium that mimics the lightness of haiku to name a few possibilities. Of course, another possibility entails combining haiku with imagery that does not attempt to comment directly upon the visual imagery created by the haiku artist but rather explores the underlying "feelings" in other visual expressions. These suggested solutions might allow the reader / viewer to experience the visual, intellectual and emotional openness of both artistic forms of expression — both independently, and in "indirect" comparison, without the one form competing with, overshadowing or directly leading / affecting the experiential and interpretative process of the reader / viewer.

The Hungarian book *MADARAK / BIRDS, 50 HAIKU* is a very attractive hardbound book (12 x 18,5 cm), with fine illustrations by visual artist Éva Pápai. The illustrations are aquarelles, sensitively executed and without too much direct interpretation of the contexts expressed in the accompanying haiku. The illustrations are consistently placed on the pages adjoining each haiku in English and in Hungarian, and the original Japanese haiku appear under each illustration. Although this attractive book is not of a standard coffee table book size, the excellent presentation enables it to function both as a work of art and as a small inspirational book that may be carried in a bag or in one's pocket so as to be read on the bus, the metro, the train ... or during a break at work or in between appointments.

One reason that the presentation achieved in this book is so successful is that the illustrations are more than mere illustrations — they are works of art which function both independently and together with the haiku, they are simple in execution and style — thus mimicking and accentuating the lightness and spontaneity and "space" of haiku as an art form, there are only two haiku translations / adaptations to the page — giving a feeling of time and space for personal reflection in a way that the language that is unimportant to the particular reader can (in fact) disappear on the page, and also because the Japanese original haiku are tastefully reproduced with calligraphy in red — thus giving a sense of writing as visual art, as well as writing and art balanced both on the illustration pages and also together with the haiku in English and in Hungarian (on the opposing pages).

In *"Voices from the Clouds"* (11 x 19 cm, softcover), there are no illustrations or works of art accompanying each haiku. There are however haiku in original Japanese, Latvian and English on each page. In my view, this small book works quite well in terms of presentation. This largely because of the excellent paper quality, the sequence and placement of haiku on each page (starting with the original haiku in Japanese in one line across the top of each page, followed by the Latvian translation / adaptation, and then with the English version on the bottom of each page), as well as the feeling of "airyness" and space created ... all of which give the book a sense of completion.

There are many memorable haiku in these two books which are both beautiful and thought-provoking. I will mention a few from each book:

from *MADARAK / BIRDS:*

Old women, pigeons,
winds and gossip
gather in this square.
                    - page 16

A wild eagle
is invited to
the room of mirrors
- page 24

Every thing will disappear:
even the rice paddy,
over it a white heron dancing
                    - page 54

To the goldcrest
every water drop
smiles
                    - page 106

and from *VOICES FROM THE CLOUDS:*

In Tokyo
The angry flower is
A snow crystal
                    - page 23

Long, long ago
A fountain
At the bottom of the sea.
                          - page 39

Walking is philosophy's
Best friend —
Voices from the clouds.
                          - page 80

Wisteria flowers
Suck in our
Sweet nothings.
                          - page 120

If I were to point out one thing that I would criticize with either of these books, it would be the consistent starting of each line with capital letters in the book *VOICES FROM THE CLOUDS*. Sometimes initial capital letters feel natural and at other times (as in these haiku) they can (in my opinion) tend to disrupt the flow and music of short literary works where lines are supposed to both function on their own and as a continuous flow. However, this is my own personal opinion and experience.

All in all, I would recommend lovers of world haiku to purchase these books, as they are quite worthy of inclusion in one's permanent collection ... for re-reading time and time again, at one's leisure.

- Adam Donaldson Powell, Oslo, 2009.

フ ゛ラックカート ゛

Balancing the Yin Against the yin

Adam Donaldson Powell

BALANCING THE YIN AGAINST THE YIN: an essay in response to Ban'ya Natuishi's "Black Card / Tarjeta negra", 169 pages, cyberwit.net, 2013, with English translations by Ban'ya Natsuishi and Eric Selling, and Spanish translations by Emilio Masià.

In "Black Card / Tarjeta negra" Ban'ya Natsuishi allows the reader to be a silent companion in his protagonist's sojourns through the the darkest side of the Yin-Yang cycle: dealing with death and loss, sorrow and disillusionment; perhaps occasionally with hints of anger or disgust, but never the less at times exhibiting an almost stoic sense of detachment, and at other times absence or resignation. And yet there is an accompanying knowledge that yin cycles are always followed by more positive and active yang cycles in the greater continuum of energy, matter, life force and Spirit.

These haiku are not so much "dark" as they are intentional explorations into the experiential darkness of brutal transformative experiences. Poets fight oppression and stalemates with their greatest sword: words. But Natsuishi - although highly-intelligent about the world and the occupation of living - is also human. He is also emotional. Words often fail to describe the depth of human emotion when spoken or written directly, without a degree of abstraction, without inculcation, and without involving or implicating our surroundings. We gain a greater sense of self-justification when we feel and can show that there is indeed chaos everywhere.

The poet's protagonist may understand that death and destruction are a part of Life, but he still feels pain. He knows that the somber clouds of disillusionment will one day be replaced by the sun rays of the yang, but he chooses to investigate in detail how the negativity besets his world and his perception of it. By recognizing this yin energy in all its manifestations and describing its core force in words, then he can possibly eventually triumph over its overwhelming force. As with most people in personal crises, it is often at some point a question of balancing the Yin against the Yin — hoping to reach a milder greyness on the path back to Light and Hope.

This book is a powerful and relentless dirge — for his parents, for victims of natural disasters and nuclear accidents, and for himself. More importantly, it is a vivid documentation of a journey through Darkness. It is private, personal ... and yet we are allowed to experience his humanness. It is not negativity but rather a beautiful account of passage through a mirror of darkness. But do not be deceived. This book was not only written for Natsuishi himself; it is written for you, me ... all of us. Perhaps it is only by connecting with the rawness of poetic emotionality that we can stop and consider the lives we are creating and the world we are destroying.

Of course, it is only human for readers to want some finalization in the denouement. But Ban'ya Natsuishi has only offered a one-way ticket. This is his journey, and his continuation is truly a new book already in the making. For now, it is just to try on his spectacles and wonder at the magnificent transference he has achieved. Just be here now — right now, and right here — with Ban'ya Natsuishi as he ponders the futility of the Black Card.

And then take your own journey — into the deeper reaches of your own emotional world and perceptions. Balance the yin against the yin. The sunlight awaits beyond the dark cloud but we must first experience and accept the inevitability of the nature of clouds.

Consider these haiku poems from the book by Ban'ya Natsuishi:

Page 57

Cloudy sky —
my own fluttering
unheard

Cielo nublado
inaudible
mi aleteo

Page 61

Torrential rain pours on
a word pursuing
a word

Bajo esta lluvia torrencial,
persigue
una palabra a la otra

Page 69

Death is not the last answer
a bird singing
behind the mountains

La muerte
no tiene la última palabra
en la recóndita sierra gorjean los pájaros

Page 70

Absence is a womb
we are traveling
to the next absence

La ausencia es un seno
somos viajeros
de la ausencia

Page 71

Ground water silently
running to a spring
a pure night wind

Fluye hacia el manantial
un cauce subterráneo
silenciosa brisa nocturna

Page 73

I throw down
a dead word
to a dead fish

Lanzo
palabras muertas
a peces muertos

Page 124

Thunderstorm
on a giant dandelion —
the silent Japanese

Rayos y truenos
sobre el gigantesco diente de león
japoneses en silencio
Page 133

This sorrow:
a broken cloud
among clouds

Esta tristeza:
nubes rotas
dentro de otra nube

Page 151

Time filled with holes
appears
in clouds filled with holes

Aparece
un tiempo agujereado
entre nubes agujereadas

- Adam Donaldson Powell, Oslo, 2016.

フ ゛ラックカート ゛

Equilibrando El Yin Contra El Yin
Adam Donaldson Powell

EQUILIBRANDO EL YIN CONTRA EL YIN: un ensayo en respuesta a Ban'ya Natuishi's "Black Card / Tarjeta negra", 169 páginas, cyberwit.net, 2013, con traducciones en inglés de Ban'ya Natsuishi y Eric Selling, y traducciones en español de Emilio Masià.

En "Black Card / Tarjeta negra" Ban'ya Natsuishi permite al lector ser un compañero silencioso en las estancias de su protagonista a través del lado más oscuro del ciclo Yin-Yang: lidiar con la muerte y la pérdida, el dolor y la desilusión; quizás ocasionalmente con indicios de enojo o disgusto, pero nunca menos exhibe a veces una sensación casi estoica de desapego, y otras veces ausencia o resignación. Y sin embargo, hay un conocimiento acompañante de que los ciclos yin siempre son seguidos por ciclos yang positivos y activos en el continuo mayor de energía, materia, fuerza vital y Espíritu.

Estos haiku no son tan "oscuros" como son exploraciones intencionales en la oscuridad experiencial de experiencias transformadoras y brutales. Los poetas combaten la opresión y los estancamientos con su mayor espada: las palabras. Pero Natsuishi - aunque altamente inteligente sobre el mundo y la ocupación de la vida - también es humano. También es emocional. Las palabras a menudo no describen la profundidad de la emoción humana cuando se habla o escribe directamente, sin un grado de abstracción, sin inculcación, y sin involucrar o implicar a nuestro entorno. Obtenemos un mayor sentido de autojustificación cuando sentimos y podemos demostrar que realmente hay caos en todas partes.

El protagonista del poeta puede entender que la muerte y la destrucción son una parte de la vida, pero él todavía siente dolor. Sabe que las sombrías nubes de desilusión serán un día reemplazadas por los rayos del sol del yang, pero él decide investigar en detalle cómo la negatividad asedia su mundo y su percepción de él. Al reconocer esta energía yin en todas sus manifestaciones y describir su fuerza central en palabras, entonces él puede eventualmente triunfar sobre su fuerza abrumadora. Como ocurre con la mayoría de las personas en crisis personales, a menudo es en algún momento una cuestión de equilibrar el Yin contra el Yin - con la esperanza de alcanzar una grisura más suave en el camino de regreso a la Luz y la Esperanza.

Este libro es un fiel poderoso e implacable - para sus padres, para las víctimas de desastres naturales y accidentes nucleares, y para sí mismo. Más importante aún, es una documentación vívida de un viaje a través de la Oscuridad. Es privado, personal ... y sin embargo se nos permite experimentar su humanidad. No es negatividad, sino más bien un hermoso relato del paso a través de un espejo de oscuridad. Pero no se deje engañar. Este libro no sólo fue escrito para Natsuishi mismo; está escrito para ti, para mí ... para todos nosotros. Tal vez sea sólo conectando con la crudeza de la emotividad poética que podemos detenernos y considerar las vidas que estamos creando y el mundo que estamos destruyendo.

Por supuesto, es sólo humano para los lectores que quieren alguna finalización en el desenlace. Pero Ban'ya Natsuishi sólo ha ofrecido un billete de ida. Este es su viaje, y su continuación es verdaderamente un nuevo libro ya en construcción. Por ahora, es sólo para probar sus gafas y maravillarse de la magnífica transferencia que ha logrado. Sólo estar aquí ahora - ahora mismo, y aquí mismo - con Ban'ya Natsuishi mientras reflexiona sobre la futilidad de la Black Card.

Y luego tomar su propio viaje - en los tramos más profundos de su propio mundo emocional y las percepciones. Equilibrar el yin contra el yin. La luz del sol espera más allá de la nube oscura, pero primero debemos experimentar y aceptar la inevitabilidad de la naturaleza de las nubes.

Considere estos poemas de haiku del libro de Ban'ya Natsuishi:

Pagina 57

Cloudy sky —
my own fluttering
unheard

Cielo nublado
inaudible
mi aleteo

Pagina 61

Torrential rain pours on
a word pursuing
a word

Bajo esta lluvia torrencial,
persigue
una palabra a la otra

Pagina 69

Death is not the last answer
a bird singing
behind the mountains

La muerte
no tiene la última palabra
en la recóndita sierra gorjean los pájaros

Pagina 70

Absence is a womb
we are traveling
to the next absence

La ausencia es un seno
somos viajeros
de la ausencia

Pagina 71

Ground water silently
running to a spring
a pure night wind

Fluye hacia el manantial
un cauce subterráneo
silenciosa brisa nocturna

Pagina 73

I throw down
a dead word
to a dead fish

Lanzo
palabras muertas
a peces muertos

Pagina 124

Thunderstorm
on a giant dandelion —
the silent Japanese

Rayos y truenos
sobre el gigantesco diente de león
japoneses en silencio

Pagina 133

This sorrow:
a broken cloud
among clouds

Esta tristeza:
nubes rotas
dentro de otra nube

Pagina 151

Time filled with holes
appears
in clouds filled with holes

Aparece
un tiempo agujereado
entre nubes agujereadas

- Adam Donaldson Powell, Oslo, 2016.

Review of "Modern Japanese Haiku", by Ban'ya Natsuishi and Sayumi Kamakura

Adam Donaldson Powell

"Modern Japanese Haiku" is yet another fine literary work by Haiku masters Ban'ya Natsuishi and Sayumi Kamakura.

I have previously had the privilege of writing a number of essays where I have commented on publications by both authors:

- in 2008: *"A modern master of haiku paints the collective conscience"* - my foreword to the English version of "Flying Pope", by Ban'ya Natsuishi, Cyberwit.net, India, 2008, pp. 139, paperback, ISBN: 978-81-8253-106-2.

- in 2008: *"CONTEMPORARY HAIKU: the renaissance and the transformation"* - literary criticism based upon "Right Eye in Twilight", published by Wasteland Press, USA, 2006, ISBN13: 978-1-60047-016-5 and ISBN10: 1-60047-016-5, 62 pages, paperback; and "Earth Pilgrimage" (Pellegrinaggio terrestre), published by Albalibri Editore, Italy, 2007, ISBN 88-89618-52-3 and ISBN 978-88-89618-52-3, 146 pages, paperback).

- in 2008: *"SAYUMI KAMAKURA: the timelessness of the veil behind the veil behind the veil"* - literary criticism based on "A Crown of Roses", a haiku collection by Sayumi Kamakura, published by Cyberwit (India), 2007, 70 pages, ISBN 978-81-8253-090-4, and "A Singing Blue: 50 Selected Haiku", published by Ginyu Press (Japan), 2000, 63 pages, ISBN 4-87944-032-9).

- in 2009: *"TWO ESSAYS ON BAN'YA NATSUISHI'S WORLD*

HAIKU", EXPRESSION OF EMOTIONS IN THE INTERNATIONAL / MULTILINGUAL HAIKU OF BAN'YA NATSUISHI" - based on "A Future Waterfall", 2004, Red Moon Press, ISBN 1-893959-46-5, USA and "Endless Helix", 2007, Cyberwit.net, ISBN 978-81-8253-072-0, India.

- *"A SHORT ESSAY ON PRESENTATION OF WORLD HAIKU"* - an essay based upon the following multilingual haiku books by Ban'ya Natsuishi: *"MADARAK / BIRDS, 50 HAIKU",* including aquarelles by Éva Pápai, translations by Ban'ya Natsuishi, Jack Galmitz and Judit Vihar, published in 2007, Balassi Kiadó, Budapest, Hungary, ISBN 978-963-506-743-5; and *"VOICES FROM THE CLOUDS",* translations by Leons Briedis, Ban'ya Natsuishi, Jim Kacian and James Shea, published in 2008, Minerva, Latvia, ISBN 978-9984-637-42-5).

- *"ESSAY ABOUT THE HAIKU PUBLISHED BY THE WORLD HAIKU ASSOCIATION - World Haiku 2008, No. 4 - a multilingual collection of contemporary haiku from around the world",* (a review of "World Haiku 2008, No. 4", published by Schichigatsudo Publishing, Tokyo, Japan, ISBN 978-4-87944-117-1, 2008, 230 pages, softcover, edited by Ban'ya Natsuishi for the World Haiku Association).

- *"Reaching towards infinity"* - Literary criticism (2009) by Adam Donaldson Powell (based upon "World Haiku 2009, No. 5", The World Haiku Association, published by Shichigatsudo, Japan, 2009, ISBN 978-4-87944-135-5, 198 pages, paperback).

It is with great pleasure that I once again have the honor and privilege of reading (and re-reading) many of the works of these two contemporary haiku masters. I include "re-reading" because some of these gems I have indeed read before. "Modern Japanese Haiku" contains 100 haiku by Ban'ya Natsuishi (excerpted from "The Diary of Everyday Hunting" (1983), "Métropolitique" (1985), "Rhythm in the Vacuum" (1986), "The Fugue of Gods" (1990), "Opera in the Human

Body" (1990), "Waves of Joy" (1992), "The Science of Megaliths and Big Trees" (1995), "Earth Pilgrimage" (1998), "Drifting" (2001), "Right Eye in Twilight" (2006), "Flying Pope: 161 Haiku" (2008), "Labyrinth of Vilnius" (2009),"Hybrid Paradise" (2010); and 100 haiku by Sayumi Kamakura (here it is not specified where these poems have been published previously but I recognize haiku from her wonderful book "A Crown of Roses" (2007)). These poems are in Japanese and in English, with English translations by Ban'ya Natsuishi, Jim Kacian, Stephen Henry Gill and James Shea.

These 100 plus 100 haiku are not billed as "The 100 best haiku of …", but rather merely as 100 Haiku, by Ban'ya Natsuishi and 100 Haiku, by Sayumi Kamakura. I consider each of their books to contain precious haiku which function excellently as both individual poems and as coordinated cogs on a wheel; a wheel that is an expression of infinity, and at the same time one of equally valid intelligence (experience) from a bird's eye perspective ("As above, so below", "outside looking in and inside looking out", etc.). All of the haiku books that I have read which have been written by these two authors, and also those edited by Ban'ya Natsuishi, are carefully envisioned, written and constructed so as to give a sense of open-ended completion, inter-connectedness, and harmony — as a whole. I do not look for "the haiku moment" in their poetry because each haiku and all of their haiku books represent (for me) "the moment", of the breath of Life becoming breathing, in all its expressions. Not one haiku is greater or lesser than the one preceding (or following) the other. Like a great work of art, literature or music, each part flows as effortlessly as any other; and there cannot be music without silences, without rhythm, without contrasts. There cannot be any "100 Best" — merely "100 Haiku".

This ability of these two haiku masters to create timelessness in a single moment is, indeed, one of my own definitions of mastery: *"The novice struggles to make pretty feet dance in the wind, while the haiku of the master yawn and stretch toward infinity … like a century-old bonsai."*

Another characteristic of a contemporary master (in any period of world history) is the ability to think outside of traditional parameters, to give new life to art forms, to explore old and new ideas from new perspectives, with variations on style, and even breaking standardized rules of technique and artistic expression. This is not so much about having a sense of rebelliousness as it is about having the courage to see with more than one's eyes, to hear noise, silence or "music" with each and every cell of your body, and to feel contact with the essence of experience without ever having to use your sense of touch. A great haiku, like any other truly great work of art, literature or music, is not forced. It is perhaps merely inhaled, and released — in a breath, as a moment.

"Modern Japanese Haiku" is a book that every haiku-lover should consider having in his or her private library. It is also a book that should be available in school curricula and in public libraries. Most importantly, it is a book that should be carried around (on your cellphone, your iPad, or in your shoulder bag or backpack) for meditation and energizing — whenever you need "a moment".

In conclusion I leave you with two haiku, each of which is, in itself, an entire book of "moments":

Finally I've noticed
a flower of melancholy
in the core of the sun

-   Ban'ya Natsuishi, from "Rhythm in the Vacuum" (1986)

A cold circle
called God
or the sun

-   Sayumi Kamakura, from "A Crown of Roses" (2007)

- Adam Donaldson Powell, Oslo, 2016.

Comments On "100 Haiku" by Ban'ya Natsuishi & Sayumi Kamakura, in Japanese and English

Adam Donaldson Powell

This small volume presents selected haiku by Ban'ya Natsuishi and Sayumi Kamakura, with excerpts from:

- Ban'ya Natsuishi's "Collected Early Haiku: Roaring River (2001), "The Diary of Everyday Hunting" (1983), "Métropolitique" (1985), "Rhythm in the Vacuum" (1986), "The Fugue of Gods" (1990), "Opera in the Human Body" (1990), "Waves of Joy" (1992), "The Science of Megaliths and Big Trees" (1995), "Earth Pilgrimage" (1998), "Drifting" (2001), "Right Eye in Twilight" (2006), "Flying Pope: 161 Haiku" (2008), "Labyrinth in Vilnius" (2009), "Hybrid Paradise" (2010) and "Black Card/Tarjeta negra" (2013); and

- Sayumi Kamakura's "A Singing Blue" (2000), "A Crown of Roses" (2007) and "Seven Sunsets" (2013).

The book highlights individual poems in small groupings, and is perhaps more light-hearted than some of Ban'ya Natsuishi's previous books. Nonetheless, these haiku poems all have levels of profundity as can be found in much of Natsuishi's work. Imagine leafing through one's memory bank of images and feelings connected with past experience — much like a photo album. Those memories and sensations that are now most subjectively vivid are not always those that we may have considered to be the most dramatic, significant or transformational at the time, but perhaps fleeting ones that we have later (now) associated with feelings, happenings and discoveries experienced recently. It is at those precious moments of protracted timeline associations that past (and sometimes seemingly forgotten) memories again come to life. They were - in fact - never really forgotten, and they may now shine anew — in a different context, sequence and perspective. In such a process — of looking back and finding new associations — we are able to see life's chain of events in a broader and more elongated line which is at once integrated and interactive. This is the calm of mature reflection, and of being able to momentarily put aside the urgency of finding permanent solutions and assessments. We must find periods of "completion" again and again before any final summation. Haiku lends itself very well to this kind of reflection, as stillness and movement often happen concurrently in the life of the haiku. Natsuishi's imagery is well-complemented by that of Kamakura. Hers is equally strong, but perhaps at times more feminine and quiet — full of harmonious color, but still emphatic.

The book is beautifully illustrated with calligraphy created by the poets themselves. The poetry and art are aesthetically presented, and in such a way so as not to compete with or cancel out one another. It is possible to reflect upon either the haiku or the illustrations, without the one being dependent upon the other. In that sense, this book qualifies as well as an art book or a coffee table book — an edition that needs space, accessibility and the "freedom" to be picked up and admired, rather than to be hidden between dozens of other books in a bookcase. It is also a book that is very conducive to reflection; one page at a sitting. As a single blade of grass holds the secrets of an entire universe, each haiku and illustration in this book can provide limitless insight into the science of living. These haiku and illustrations are alive.

This book contains no foreword, and no explanation stating the intentions of the authors. None is needed as the book speaks quite well for itself. The reader is quickly plunged into the minds, senses and sensibilities of the two haiku masters, without preparation or expectation. It is at once both *zazen* and walking meditation. There is no need to follow our breathing or rid ourselves of competing thoughts, as the authors' "music" synchronizes our sensibilities, rhythms and sensations with that of their own.

-Adam Donaldson Powell, Oslo, 2016.

Voices from the Clouds
Aiswarya T Anish

Haiku is not just the broken-up three lines of emotions that studies of haiku have told us it is about. Just type in the word 'haiku' on the internet and one gets all he needs to know: explanations and criticism, examples and instructions on writing haiku. There are hundreds, perhaps thousands of poets, who have tried their hand at haiku. But it is only a few who have been able to master the art of writing a perfect haiku. Ban'ya Natsuishi is one such poet who has exceptional mastery over haiku, making his haiku stand alongside the ones by great masters such as Kobayashi Issa and Matsuo Basha.

While reading Ban'ya Natsuishi, it is difficult to determine whether we are reading poetry or whether we are reliving, revelling in those forgotten instances of nostalgia. His haiku evinces an unusual amount of sympathy, satisfaction and yearning- all those qualities which make us so utterly human. Just as much as Ban'ya's haiku soothes us at times, it unsettles us. It disturbs us, makes us think because of the wealth of contrasts and paradoxes in his lines.

Ban'ya's greatest possession is perhaps his gift for simplicity. Even the most intense of emotions are put out to us without the haggling of harsh, complex vocabulary, nevertheless keeping all of the feeling and intensity of emotions in the few words that he does use to convey his thoughts. In *Modern Japanese Haiku*, a collection of haiku by Ban'ya and Sayumi Kamukara, the haiku contains more vivid and violent imagery. Many talk about blood and death, about destruction and melancholy.

Cherry blossoms fall:

Newspapers

Suck in a great deal of blood

In the above haiku, we begin with a symbolism of hope and humility-the cherry blossom. We think about spring, we think of the tree which is about to bear fruit and suddenly, without warning, we see the newspapers. We see the disturbing image of newspapers drenched in a fiery liquid. We see them "suck in a great deal of blood". Ban'ya can ambush the unsuspecting reader with such unexpected contrasts, he can juxtapose a cherry blossom with a blood stained newspaper to make the former look so fragile and simple or the latter so violent and terrible than it already is. Or he can simple make us unsettled. Disturb us. Make us hunt for answers. At times, he examines beauty through not a description of the sight but of the reaction, or the surge of emotions caused by it.

Cherry in bloom —
the task of stopping the breath
finished

If the cherry blossoms in the first haiku were the silent witness of violence and melancholy, the one here is a wonder to behold. Ban'ya in is three lines is able to catch the splendour of the cherry tree by telling us about the reaction it causes. We can 'feel' our breath stopping, and at the same time the cause for it- a cherry tree in bloom.

Ban'ya experiments. He is brave enough to stray away from the 5-7-5 syllable structure to do what he wills with his words and emotions. He shows us that great poetry is not just the ones that moulds and prunes itself to fit into a pre-defined syllabic framework. He lets his magic twist and turn and transforms these three-line skeletons into clouds and curlicues, into heroes and helixes. In essence, Ban'ya doesn't just write poetry, he gives it life.

Watching
surreal clouds
I'm on my way back to a tiny house

This sorrow:
a broken cloud
among clouds

My father's eyes
are my grandfather's eyes
ripples in their depths

The above haiku are examples of his talent in the craft of exceptional poetry. Ban'ya makes us fall in love with this art-form. He makes us nostalgic as we look at the surreal clouds; he sends a pang through our hearts as he talks about a broken cloud, ripples in our conscience as we think of our own fathers and grandfathers. As we read Ban'ya, we see through his eyes, we hear voices from the clouds he sits on, we see Tokyo and the people in it, we see outside the city to grab at the mysteries of the universe. And through our course of reading, we watch in awe as:

A glass dragonfly
becomes a ball of fire
takes a tour of Tokyo

***

Ban'ya Natsuishi,
Haiku Unresembling
Amitabh Mitra

The universal rule of Haiku is 5, 7, 5 syllables in three lines. I as a poet and a visual artist have delved into Banya's creativity and found utmost pleasure.

From here onwards I shall refer them as poems and words imprinted in abstract colors. Each of these three lines and sometimes even one line makes me read them again because each time, they come to us in a different beauty, different understanding.

Banya and the 21st century with its politics, war, struggle for survival and genocide which the global contemporary poetry movement is surging in an iconoclast explosion, his words are a release, a catharsis from sorrow and torture.

Within his Hybrid Forest –

Within a Tokyo forest
a stray man runs into
a stray man

The beauty of these lines are caressed by the stark darkness of poverty

Great inebriation deepens
our memories–
our days toward death

Banya cleverly chastens the subtlety of death

Talking of poetry
time disappears
leaves grow

Banya strums the strings of a guitar, poetry springs to shape

It would be nearly impossible to give a critical viewpoint of Banya's works because they don't resemble anybody. The body of Banya;s works if taken together and let his words scatter, each of them will still form a poem with the other

I am not a spiritual person yet I do believe in the mysticism of the mind. The mind is an aura, it regulates the human physiology and beyond. Impenetrable and Inaccessible as it is, its creation of inexhaustible words that may or may not have any relation to each other but eventually allows a colorful thought, is the magic of Banya's creation.

Post war Japan and Banya's creativity: I believe beyond the trauma existing in every Japanese mind, young or old, till even today, there also flows a struggle to create identities, possibilities and realities. Banya's work shows a constant shift of landscapes that undo the past and present. The realm of forest overshadowing Banya's poetry is further consistent with realizing of the eternal sky and the mind where a flower blossoms. Banya holds hope in fragrance and cherry flowers, in stray men lost in magical forests, in surrealist attitudes that defy the ever changing color.

I believe the powerful impact of Banya's short poems, not necessarily Haiku are profound, they talk about the fifth dimension where mind merges with space, life continues to be a perennial flower.

I quote from my book of poems, touched by Banya's work

Eternity has space
Eternity has a flower

Ban'ya Natsuishi:
The Haikuist of Our Age
Anna Cates

To most serious Haikuists, Ban'ya Natsuishi is a familiar name. Natsuishi is a professor at Meiji University, Director of the World Haiku Association, president of Ginyu Press, and Director of Tokyo Poetry Festival. Those haikuists who've submitted poems to the acclaimed poet/publisher/editor may recall the affectionate "Love ya" with which Natsuishi concludes his personal correspondences. And those who've taken the time, or had the opportunity, to enjoy Natsuishi's creative works may have noted and been impressed by the emotional depth in his poetry. This emotional depth is one of the primary characteristics of Natsuishi's writing that sets him apart and lends to his verse its distinctive strength. Let's take a closer look at representative haiku from three of his highly acclaimed books: *Endless Helix*, *Hybrid Paradise*, and *Black Card*.

ENDLESS HELIX:

In *Endless Helix* (2009) Natsuishi presents haiku evoking a wide range of emotions. From love to fear, from longing to grief, Natsuishi's selections reflect the human condition in their depth of feeling.

With her child

my sister returns home —

a peach tree in full bloom (25)

In this selection, we find the simple theme of family. The child reflects the promise of life's continuity, symbolized by a fruit bearing tree in full bloom, connected to the child. The poem is uplifting, evoking emotions of love and joy.

Longing is another emotion evoked in selections within *Endless Helix*.

The bird wants

to become a black stone

in the bosom of the moon (26)

In this selection, Natsuishi projects unfulfilled human desire onto the bird. The poem concerns unutterable human longing that can be referenced only metaphorically as the "black stone / in the bosom of the moon." Perhaps significantly, the moon is personified, reflecting the human wish for intimacy.

Fear is another emotion evoked in many of Natsuishi's selections from the same volume.

From a cloud

the silver-haired demon

roars with laughter (15)

Stylistically, poems of this caliber may harken back to Japan's artistic tradition, with painters such as Kawanabe Kyosai (see figure 1), whose works were laden with ghosts and demons, depicting human fears difficult to express with words, fears of death and the supernatural unknown.

Figure 1: Art by Kawanabe Kyosai

The poem remains open-ended. It could express a child's innocent fear of a thunderstorm or the more sinister reality of the nuclear mushroom cloud, the latter theme more directly presented in some of Natsuishi's other poems. The possibility of the poet depicting a more innocent, childhood memory of his own fear appears in other selections from the collection, as noted below:

> High waves
>
> remind me of my father
>
> dead drunk (36)

Here the poet may be sharing with us of the difficulties of his childhood: a father who sometimes drank to excess and the unfading memories of the fearful emotions it produced. Of course, the poem is also analogous, speaking directly of a tsunami's menacing threat.

Uncertainly is another emotion evoked with depth by selections within *Endless Helix*.

> The gold and black
>
> in the picture —
>
> which is our future? (12)

Here, the poet uses color to symbolize negative and positive outcomes. What does our future hold? Good or bad? Gold or black? The anxiety caused by such uncertainties is successfully suggested through figurative language.

> Below is another selection evoking a feeling of uncertainty.
>
> A cloud beyond any shape —
>
> we have lost
>
> our memory (35)

This selection's import is highly open-ended. Many different possibilities for interpretation are inherent through association. Might the poet speak of the possibility of dementia in old age? Or does he call to mind our human inability, or belligerent refusal, to learn from the mistakes of our past? Either way, the feeling of uncertainly comes across clearly through the poet's careful diction and imagery.

Natsuishi also grapples with feelings of sorrow and grief in *Endless Helix*.

The snake has stolen
the golden grass:
our first unhappiness (24)

The poet speaks of that unhappy moment we might experience when we find we've lost something precious, and we don't understand how it happened! The golden grass metaphorically presents that precious thing. The snake, harkening back to Christian archetype and myth, is that ambiguous evil that thwarts us.

Grief over loss is also evoked in the following selection:

Where there was a tree
near the pure spring—
the noise of saws (8)

True, haiku often deals with naturalistic themes so that deforestation itself would amount to a woe worth lamenting. Yet an additional metaphorical level is possible. The tree may represent that element worth preserving that becomes lost through destruction.

Another selection that depicts grief caused by death or destruction, more clearly in this instance, can be noted below:

The word "Hiroshima"
is it heavier
than a butterfly? (9)

Here, Natsuishi uses the rhetorical device of questioning to prompt our thinking about an important topic of emotional impact.

Some of the deepest feelings evoked in the volume involve a horror produced by apprehension over death.

Far from his homeland
the skull is a villa
for a snake (21)

The poet uses skillful strategies to evoke feelings of grief over the loss of a loved one. A personal pronoun, "his," is used to describe a skull that was once a living being, affectionately held. Compounding and deepening the emotion is the snake; that archetypical, evil enemy of man; who's taken over and now possesses all that's left of the deceased person. The living snake writhing in the skull is more horrible than an empty skull. This is another selection that may harken back to Japan's artistic tradition, with painters such as Kawanabe Kyosai (see figure 2).

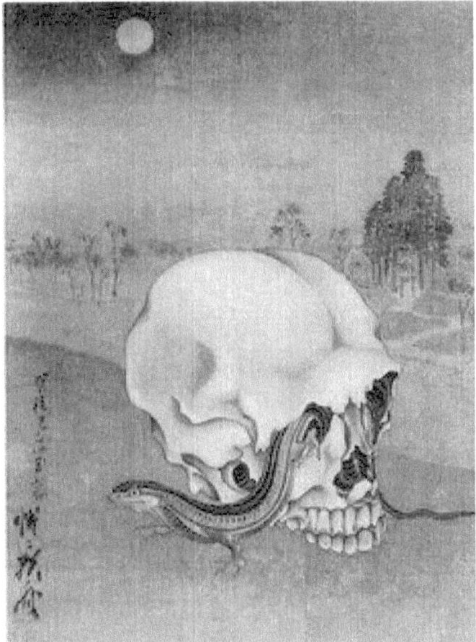

Figure 2: Art by Kawanabe Kyosai

HYBRID PARADISE:

Natsuishi's style of writing haiku with emotional depth continues in *Hybrid Paradise* (2010). Compared to his earlier works, haiku in *Hybrid Paradise* are also deeply emotionally evocative and introduce new themes and feelings.

One may note the sense of futility captured in the below selection.

A great decision on Monday
roses
blown by a wind (4)

Here we get the sense that all our plans, symbolized by the roses, will be lost by upheavals beyond our control. Natsuishi conveys the idea of tragedy subtly through natural imagery.

With all the death and disaster resulting from hurricanes, Tsunamis, and nuclear disasters, separation anxiety is another emotion the poet artfully conveys:

Between father and me
mountains, rivers
and cities of fire (86)

Here, the poet continues the naturalistic tradition in haiku, using natural images to convey human emotion, linking human experience with nature.

The same strategy can be noted in the below selection, expressing the feeling of dehumanization.

Within a Tokyo forest
a stray man runs into
a stray man (4)

Ironically, the "forest" in this instance may be merely the asphalt jungle, while men are compared to dogs. Natsuishi suggests things haven't changed—we haven't progressed from our primordial past—we're trapped in primitive, animalistic existence.

We see the same idea hinted at in another selection.

During an earthquake
a monkey keyboarding
in Japan (10)

The impact of natural disasters have dehumanized or devolved us. Nature has put us back in our place. Now, we remain like caged animals:

Red tears

black blood

our language is a cage (38)

This selection evokes a feeling of confinement. We become slaves to a clean up after the natural disaster. Startling colors heighten the emotion inherent in the imagery.

A sense of being confined or constricted emerges in other selections as well, as multiple haiku converge thematically to enhance the emotional impact of each other.

Words and glances:

waves

within this box (9)

Here, life following the disaster is like living in a tiny box. We are caged; we are trapped; all we do and say is restricted to a tiny space, bounded on every side by impenetrable walls. Line two may hint with more particularity at the nature of the disaster: a raging sea. Natsuishi clarifies the experience through the crafting technique of association (Reichhold).

The poet succeeds in depicting the apocalyptic experience with appropriate depth.

Bread and light

an inch away

from a doghouse (108)

Here, continuing with the concept of dehumanization, the poet uses irony and imagery to describe a famished human being, inching toward the comfort of a bowl of dog's food. The image is startling, presenting one vivid example of the terrible impact of natural and/or nuclear disaster.

The poet uses metaphor effectively to convey the impact of the apocalypse.

Violent wind —
a thousand mice
pushing a car of fire (89)

Once more, humankind, grappling with natural and/or nuclear disaster, is dehumanized into the tiniest of creatures, striving beneath impossible burdens.

However, though many of the poet's emotions and themes are dark in this volume, he also includes selections expressive of hope and joy.

Cherry blossoms never fallen
in the castle of our heart
here is a path (30)

In this poem, the hopeful speaker tenaciously holds one, finding within himself something with which to carry on. That life also provides joy is overtly expressed in another selection as well.

In the middle of jet lag
a great joy
like deep sea water (63)

Here, the poet expresses that moment in which happiness bubbles up within him for no particular reason. It is a shared human experience the reader can comprehend and relate to.

BLACK CARD:

Black Card (2013) may be Natsuishi's darkest collection, yet, arguably, the one most in need of being read. The haiku in this collection center most definitively on urban upheaval after tsunami and nuclear disaster and the utter insecurity and abject horror of being caught in such catastrophes. As the reality of the potential for these disasters cannot be denied, it remains for the reader a topic worthy of exploration, with Natsuishi's poetry comprising an excellent vehicle toward that end.

In *Black Card*, the poet depicts with great emotional depth a climate of physical and metaphysical desolation after calamity. Moreover, he uses a variety of poetic strategies to create depth of feeling. Personification and animation are several literary devices he employs.

Fukushima fire

bares its fangs

water weeping (79)

Here the nuclear disaster is demonized, while human grief and despair is projected onto nature, deepening the emotion.

Natsuishi uses irony and religious allusion to express his grief over devastated nature:

Grass bud

richly baptized

by plutonium (89)

In this selection, focusing on a single blade of grass, the poet employs the haiku crafting technique of "thinking small" and "looking closely" as an approach to depicting one scene or "aha moment" (Janeczko 52). Also, by employing ironic word choices such as "richly baptized," which normally have positive connotations, to portray nuclear contamination, the poet enhances the emotional impact of the poem. He makes light of the situation, almost satirically. This is a poetic technique understood to evoke emotion (Hambrick 1).

Natsuishi employs the same strategy of ironic diction in additional selections.

Accidental festival of anxiety

in front of a station

after an earthquake (76)

The poet uses unexpected and fresh word choices such as "festival" to describe the horror. Irony, "when the unexpected happens, or is said," is another poetic technique known to evoke emotion (Hambrick 1).

In other instances, the poet astonishes us to enhance the emotional impact.

Behind a vacant tower

mold

on dog shit (64)

The reader is presented with one layer of the grotesque on top of another, as the poet continues to "look closely" and "think small."

The power of the tsunami is effectively depicted, along with the emotional impact to the beholder, in the following selection.

A giant tsunami

gives birth to

a waterfall of cars (82)

The poet employs vivid exemplification and specificity to deepen the poem's emotional impact.

Natsuishi uses the rhetorical strategy of comparison and contrast to compare the devastation of the disaster to a feeling of being unloved.

No love:

a giant tongue of waves

licking everything (77)

This technique of comparison is intrinsic to haiku, and Natsuishi does it expertly. As noted by Betty Drevniok: "In haiku the SOMETHING and the SOMETHING ELSE are set down together in clearly stated images. Together they complete and fulfill each other as ONE PARTICULAR EVENT" (Reichhold).

With vivid imagery and synesthesia, the perception that one physical stimulus is another, (Trumball 101) Natsuishi depicts the tragedy of death.

Singing stars

over the gently sloping road

toward death (41)

The poet makes death personal and undignified, depicting his father with personal parts exposed and "open":

My father, mouth

and anus wide open —

a shining cloud (44)

Vivid images such as these are always emotionally evocative. As noted by Lee Gurga, imagery involves both "an intuitive and *emotional complex*" (emphasis added) related to the "aha moment."

However, despite the darkness and horror of *Black Card*, the volume also depicts hope, providing a broader range of emotions.

Death is not the last answer

a bird singing

behind the mountains (69)

Here, the idea of life after death in introduced metaphorically. The singing bird is like our soul, finding paradise "behind the mountains." Again, the poet masterly applies his crafting techniques, as metaphor is a device useful to generate feeling (Ross).

Towards the end of the volume, many of the selections transition to religious, particularly Christian, allusions.

Watch again

Jesus's despair

made of rocks (156)

These "Christian" haiku are more hopeful, hinting at redemption, reflective of a poet open-mindedly searching for answers to difficult questions.

Overall, in *Black Card*, the poet presents Japan's recent natural and nuclear disasters as taking on dimensions beyond the physical or natural. A supernatural, metaphysical aspect is embedded in the tragedies, leaving the poet grappling on multiple levels. Using a variety of crafting strategies to foster depth of emotion, Natsuishi gives those lucky enough to not have personally witnesses the apocalyptic events a chance to understand and learn from them.

Natsuishi achieves depth of emotion, and a variety of emotions, in his haiku by employing diverse poetic techniques. He succeeds poetically by evoking emotion within the reader rather than by merely expressing emotion as self-centered venting. As Lee Gurga relays:

Look at the finest of the classics and the finest contemporary haiku and I believe you will find a common thread – characterised (sic) as having a dedication to truthfulness combined with a lack of self-consciousness. Northrop Frye wrote that, 'The poet's task is to deliver the poem in as uninjured a state as possible, and if the poem is alive, it is equally anxious to be rid of him, and screams to be cut loose from his private memories and associations, his desire for self-expression, and all the other navel-strings and feeding tubes of his ego.' [1] This is the kind of haiku that I appreciate.

By attending to the reader's needs rather than fixating on his own psyche, Natsuishi's poems achieve their imperishable quality. "Meaningful poems invite or evoke an emotional response" (Hambrick 1). With their depth of emotion, Natsuishi's haiku is truly meaningful.

Works Cited

Gurga, Lee. "New Zealand Poetry Society Te Hunga Tito Ruri O Aotearoa." *Toward an*

Aesthetic for English-Language Haiku by Lee Gurga. Web. 30 Sept. 2015. <http://www.poetrysociety.org.nz/node/323>.

Hambrick, Willow. "The Poem as Craft: Poetic Elements." Web.

<https://english.as.uky.edu/sites/default/files/ThePoemAsCraft_byWillowHambrick.pdf>.

Janeczko, Paul. *How to Write Haiku and Other Short Poems*. New York: Scholastic, 2004. Print.

Kyosai, Kawanabe, 2 Oct. 2015

< http://kyosai-museum.jp/Mvc013fc.jpg>.

Kysoai, Kawanabe, 2 Oct. 2015

< https://s-media-cache-ak0.pinimg.com/236x/3e/f0/9a/ 3ef09aa5471e06966294042a371fdc8e.jpg >.

Natsuishi, Ban'ya. *Endless Helix*. 2nd. ed. Allahabad: Cyberwit.net, 2009. Print.

Natsuishi, Ban'ya. *Hybrid Paradise*. Allahabad: Cyberwit.net, 2010. Print.

Natsuishi, Ban'ya. *Black Card*. Allahabad: Cyberwit.net, 2013. Print.

Reichhold, Jane. "Haiku Techniques." *Frogpond* (Autumn 2000). Web. 1 Oct. 2015.

< http://www.ahapoetry.com/haiartjr.htm >.

Ross, Bruce. "The Essence of Haiku." *Modern Haiku* 38.3 (2007). Web. 1 Oct. 2015. <http://www.modernhaiku.org/essays/ RossEssenceHaiku.html>.

Trumball, Charles. "Meaning in Haiku." *Frogpond* 35.3 (2012): 92-118. Print.

Haiku by Ban'ya Natsuishi
Kalyan Panja

Haroldo de Campos, the great Brazilian poet, scholar of medieval romance tradition, often said that the only way to really respect the tradition was to renew it, put it back into play, and make them live new adventures, because the only way to reaffirm the importance of a rule is to violate it, by changing its meaning, without misinterpretation.

Haiku, as we used to read it, no longer exists, disfigured by an enormous creative force that remodels and scramble a tradition because this can return to recognize in it is unquestionably a sign of true poetry. The haiku is a kind of short poem born in Japan in the 17th century, composed of three lines, respectively of 5-7-5 syllables originally a form used to express the emotions aroused by the nature and seasonal changes, to which the Japanese are particularly sensitive.

But over time, even in Japan, haiku has taken on a less specific meaning and now simply indicates a form of poetry extremely short, well-defined by the metric. How do you explain the success of this particular form of poetry as in the West? It is a process that began in the 19th century, when the Western conception of art and literature suffered the influences of Eastern thought.

Moreover, in recent years, it has added an intense reflection on the relationship between man and nature that has landed in all unusual positions from the nature, traditional theme of haiku, with blunt accents. The process is radicalized even more, with the anaphoric return of the same protagonist, where it is not difficult to grasp the stylization that causes the individual poetic frames, even with their apparent autonomy, constitute a loose-knit narrative, of course, but even with its obvious solid plot, since it is entirely new and surprising haiku.

The result is a real gem of contemporary Japanese haiku, suffice it to mention some of the many pieces that make up this surreal quasi-poem and make it look like a sarcastic band. It has bewitched the audience with the brief and scathing lyrics, poems of only three verses dedicated to the places visited during its travels around the world.

Call them pilgrimages, because they aim to spread the "poetic word" in the five continents. But what is haiku to Ban'ya Natsuishi? It is the poetic form who at the age of 15 chose to express himself which conquered him, as a boy, with its brevity, its ability to convey strong emotions in a few words, and constitute a kind of puzzle to solve.

I think for example to the Impressionists, Van Gogh, and for their paintings was inspired by Japanese art. But also to the avant-garde poets, Thomas Stearns Eliot in "Wasteland", and Ezra Pound, who was among the first to use haiku while writing in English. With the Dadaists and Surrealists poetry soon spread to France, until it lands in the 20th century, in Mexico and Greece.

To attract Western poets was certainly the conciseness of haiku, its fragmentation, and the sense of mystery inherent in a lyric so short, and the ability to encompass a whole world in words measured with the dropper. It was a big change for Western writers, who until then had favoured the long forms of poetry, the rooms, and the sonnets.

I do not think too much to dare say that Haroldo would definitely have appreciated haiku of prestigious scholar and expert Ban'ya Natsuishi, because the Japanese author put back into the haiku the famous ruthless twist to a Japanese manner. This makes sharp tool of analysis of a reality that, for its part, seems made to deny the very roots of haiku.

Ban'ya used haiku as a crowbar to open gaps in cultural existential geography of countries and cultures near and far, from Rome and Genoa, to New York and India, with a style that can ignite whipping controversy and ominously prophetic visions. The contemptuous irony, or the ability to grasp the hidden folds in which is hidden the key to understanding this or that moment, build a travel story in which each haiku becomes the frame of a film almost à la Godard.

Contemporary Haiku by Ban'ya

Malini

Ban'ya's collection is contemporary Haiku that weaves in aspects of nature albeit with an irony attached. It is expansive in terms of subject choices and lends more to a fabulous reading experience.

I am choosing to describe some of his works that I personally find interesting and worth reflecting upon.

Within a Tokyo forest
A stray man runs into
A stray man

This is a very apt example of contemporary haiku. Nature woven in on the sly but the irony of our world shines out. Here Tokyo a rather busy city has been compared to a forest and man has been described as a wanderer akin to an animal lost in this forest. I find the juxtaposition simple yet very powerful. It leaves me feeling one with the Haiku. A reflection our day to day life.

Perhaps the strongest of Haiku written by Ban'ya are the ones that deal with contemporary issues, the trials and travails of our lives today. Nature plays an interesting role in all Ban'ya's Haiku.

Distorted and vanished
Printed monkeys
And cyber monkeys

Technology juxtaposed with nature a comparison of the human ape with the monkey and then the words 'distorted and vanished' are powerful and give you a peek into the poet's mind.

Another example that depicts the irony of our world today is:

Far East
Roads opened
Doors closed

I especially like the simplicity of vocabulary in Ban'ya's Haiku. He is not pretentious and says what he needs to say with candor in easy to connect with language. Yet each Haiku leaves a lasting indelible impression on the mind.

The loneliness of human beings is depicted beautifully in this Haiku. Where on the one hand the technological advancements are connecting cities and towns, people are becoming more and more disconnected due to self-inflicted loneliness.

Another one from the Dragon Shadow section that leaves a lasting impression on the mind is

Carrying a poetess Mary
And her chronic illnesses
The plane is heavy

The depiction of endlessness of poetry and the mortality of human beings in this piece is compelling and starkly morose. The word heavy is effective and evokes a dark emotion. It is as if the timelessness of poetry and mortality of the poet are weighing heavily on the plane, which seems to be filled with sorrow. Plane here becomes an alive, aware part of the Haiku.

I find Ban'ya is a highly observant poet. He catches a glimpse of the ordinary happening and turns them into extraordinary philosopies.

The station square in summer
My aunt lamenting
Very slowly

This is a marvelous contrast. Busy station square scene and eyes that have seen everything move at contrasting paces from eachother. One creates a sense of urgency to reach somewhere and the other defies the urgency of the world, knowing the futility of the rush (lamenting very slowly).

Hybrid Paradise section has a haiku:

My words and black teeth
Lit up
They are hybrid

Self explanatory but powerful in today's context, this haiku is apt as an example of juxtaposition or as the section suggests hybrid paradise.

A crane in the background
Talk of ugliness
A new elegance

This is a direct take on pretensions in today's world. We are missing the beauty (crane in the background) around us and looking for ugly spots and focusing on those. This is interestingly true about how media portrays everything too. We are becoming a pessimistic people in the garb of intellectual realists.

A flower field
Within a sick room
"No Visitors"

This Haiku is again a reminder of the loneliness even in death or similar predicament. A subtle hint at the busy life all around us comes across right at the beginning (a flower field within a sick room). It means there are enough number of people that are aware and connected with us but none is available to share our loneliness with.

The sun gives a kiss
To books
Piled up

I personally love this Haiku. I will start with usage of 'piled up.' This creates a picture of neglect. Books become alone and neglected alive things that await a kind word or tender care and yet only the Sun cares to give them a kiss. This is a beautiful Haiku.

Above a Giant Wheel
We are talking of world haiku
Flowerily

I would like to think of the Giant Wheel as earth that rotates on its own axis with all of us taking our ride. Discussing world Haiku is like discussing different lives, poetry, philosophies at the same time carefully so as to not hurt sentiment of one another (flowerily) even though we may have a different point of view altogether.

Sound of rain unheard
A temporary deathbed
On the 5th floor

This is a wonderful example of 'show, don't tell' form of Haiku. Ban'ya creates an image that shows the restrictive nature of mortality and death. Infact death is a very beautifully handled subject by Ban'ya.

Wind
carrying away clouds
A pump near the death bed

My gold fish doing a headstand
In summer is his
Farewell posture

These two Haiku not only create an image in the readers mind but also use metaphors enhancing the meaning.

'Wind carrying away clouds' depicts the powerful force of nature. 'A pump near the death bed' explains how binding nature will still not absolve us of our mortal state.

Similarly a change of season has been used lightly to discuss change. The fish dies in summer but the words used to describe its death are 'farewell posture', bringing mortality to us more as change than death and a definite end.

Whilst Ban'ya paints a lovely picture with each Haiku he is a master of satire too. Aware of his politics he comes up with some interesting work signifying his dislike for political games.

A chair is creaking

A crazy election

In a crazy season of rain

Chaos (election) upon chaos (rain) for a chair is a clear inference one can draw. The usage of crazy before election and season of rain is where Ban'ya excels as a poet. He uses these words to add to the drama around the election time and calls it senseless.

Ban'ya is critical of the state of affairs and where this world is headed. His bias against nuclear energy sources and man's habit of repeating mistakes is evident in Haiku written post the Tsunami misfortune in Japan.

Grass bud

Richly baptized

By plutonium

and

Human Singularity

Pollutes

Plurality of Gods

Destruction of the world is the clear message conveyed in both the above Haiku. Ban'ya is critical of the state of affairs and condemns the usage of nuclear energy that can destroy all life forms on earth. All it takes is a Tsunami (Nature's wrath) to bring mankind to its knees. Usage of the words Singularity and Plurality are exceptional. Singularity (conveying both usage of nuclear energy and mankind's selfish nature) and Plurality (diversity in nature) are clever words to convey a serious message. Here Ban'ya's angst is evident.

Similarly his Haiku below:

Sixty Six Year after Japan's defeat
White smoke
From a nuclear reactor

This is another great example of his frustration against mankind. Inspite of the disastrous effects of Hiroshima Nagasaki, Japan decided to go the nuclear way and created another such situation with the Fukushima reactor leak. He is telling us that mankind has not learnt anything from its own mistakes in the past.

Not only does Ban'ya speak of the east. He is abreast with the goings on in other parts of the world.

The state of poverty in Nigeria and the government's mandate to provide electricity and the actuality of the ground level situation has been described well in this Haiku.

Electricity passed by
A hut with a bamboo-covered roof
Without dropping in

Overall I think Haiku is more than a form of poetry it is a way of seeing the world and Ban'ya succeeds at doing just that.

Each of his haiku captures a moment of experience, an instant when the ordinary suddenly reveals its inner nature and makes us take a second look at the event, at human nature, at life, reveling in beauty or acknowledging the ugly. What Ban'ya does is he makes us pause and take notice, and recall them hours later, the feeling of having had a momentary insight transcending the ordinary.

Ban'ya Natsuishi's Revelations from the Everyday

Marta Knobloch

"—one principal purpose of haiku is to discover something new in the everyday and to reveal it to the world—" from the speech given by Ban'ya Natsuishi for the Lahti International Writers' Reunion, 2009

Black Card is a tri-lingual (Japanese, Spanish and English) collection of haiku by Ban'ya Natsuishi published by Cyberwit.net in 2013. The range of the 234 haiku in the book is sweeping enough to include poems inspired by the tsunami followed by the nuclear cataclysm that struck Japan in 2011 and the universal trauma of the death of a parent. His emotional response to the impact of both of these momentous events has resulted in powerful work filled with startling images.

"Tsunami & Nuclear Reactor" is a group of poems Natsuishi wrote after the earthquake and tsunami that devastated Japan on March 11, 2011. As a result, the cooling system of the Fukushima Daiichi Nuclear Power Plant failed and a level-7 nuclear meltdown occurred. This catastrophe caused the deaths of over fifteen thousand people and there are thousands still missing.

Nuclear reactors

on the island of earthquakes and tsunamis

cherry blossom in full bloom

The recurrent natural disasters of "earthquakes and tsunamis" in Japan, an island nation, are an ever-present threat to a "cherry blossom in full bloom," an enduring metaphor for the fragility of life in traditional haiku. The poet contends constructing "nuclear reactors" in such an unstable environment reveals irresponsibility bordering on rashness.

Windy streets
cedar pollen and radioactivity
flying over them

The "windy streets" in the first line of this haiku echo the bleakness of a nuclear winter. "Cedar pollen and radioactivity" are the results of two manmade calamities. Reforestation on a massive scale by planting only Japanese cedar to replace oak, maple and other indigenous trees has resulted in the lowering of the water table, the decimation of wildlife, and massive landslides due to soil erosion. Clouds of pollen released by cedar forests in the spring cause pollenosis and other respiratory allergies that affect one-tenth of the Japanese population. Radioactive isotopes were released during the nuclear meltdown of the Fukushima Daiichi Power Plant. They were still detectable in sea water in 2014 and 2015. "Flying over" those dismal streets is the ominous specter of an age filled with the unimagined consequences of misguided government policies which seek to manipulate the natural environment.

A giant tsunami
gives birth to
a waterfall of cars

This haiku reminds me of a painting by Salvador Dali .[1] Although the image of a mammoth wave cresting and then crashing down in "a waterfall of cars" is based in fact, it is as surreal as a nightmare. One pictures little boys' toy cars superimposed on Hosukai's famous wood print "The Giant Wave of Kanawaga."[2] That the tsunami "births" cars suggests the ineffectual childishness of our modern world's reaction when faced with a disaster of such magnitude.

One shaking invites another
a glass of vanity
falling down

A society shaken by the terrible destruction resulting from the Tohoku earthquake, tsunami and nuclear meltdown looks at itself in a "glass of vanity" which has become a shattered mirror. Robert

Oppenheimer, the American physicist known as the Father of the Atomic Bomb, said after the first successful nuclear test, "I remembered the line from the Hindu scripture, the *Bhagavad-Gita*, 'Now I am become death, the destroyer of worlds.'"[3] Natsuishi "invites" us to reflect on our hubris, our playing with the fire of the gods which could result in a punishment as horrible as that of Prometheus.[4]

The haiku in "One Cloud to Another" are a part of the collection that was written after the death of the poet's father. They express with unadorned candor the intensely felt sorrow of losing a parent.

> My father's eyes
> are my grandfather's eyes
> ripples in their depths

When Natsuishi gazes into his "father's eyes," he is reminded of his "grandfather's eyes" and how these two iconic figures have been of central importance in his life. Even at this wrenching time of parting there is the comforting sense of family continuity. His father and grandfather will live on in his memories of them.

> His whole face smiling
> in a hospital room –
> only this miracle

Natsuishi is deeply moved that his father's "whole face" is "smiling" even though he is in a "hospital room." It is a "miracle" that he smiles at his son as he himself is passing beyond illness and pain. They can share this wondrous moment of grace.

> Mournful loss!
> a limitless slanted line
> a cherry petal

The poet mourns the death of his father with a grief that is overwhelming. The "limitless slanted line" could be an allusion to the endless downward slope of death or an oblique reference to the flat line that appears on the screen of a monitor after the heart ceases to beat.

Fallen cherry blossoms have historically been symbolically associated with mortality in Japanese literature and art. "A cherry petal" is Natsuishi's graceful epitaph for his father, expressing the beauty and sadness of life's ephemerality.

> Our feelings
>
> have no right answer
>
> the blue sky

The poet knows that neither defiance nor acquiescence brings solace when facing death. We are unable to penetrate its mystery. We are left with the emptiness of "the blue sky," the infinite void. As Hamlet tells us in his final speech, "The rest is silence."[5]

> On the cross road of souls
>
> watch and clock
>
> must disappear

The translation of the Japanese phrase "mono no aware" in English is "the pathos of things." It indicates the sad acceptance of knowing all things must end, that this is our fate and the fate of the world. Everything ends. Natsuishi poignantly illuminates this somber realization in this haiku.

The poet has said, "My concern is not expressing emotion in a new way, but something deeper than emotion is my target."[6] In his endeavor to give voice to the ineffable, his poems often resonate with that which is inexpressible, but profound and transcendent. It is this resonance that the reader perceives and responds to in Natsuishi's poetry.

Works Cited

1. Salvatore Dali (May 11, 1904 - January 23, 1989) was a famous Spanish surrealist painter.

2. Katsushika Hokusai (October 31, 1760 – May 10, 1849) was a Japanese artist whose most famous work is the woodblock print, *The Great Wave of Kanawaga.*

3. J. Robert Oppenheimer (April 12, 1904 – February 18, 1967) was an American physicist who headed The Manhattan Project which created the first nuclear weapons during World War II.

4. In one of the Greek myths Prometheus stole fire from the gods to benefit mankind. Zeus punished him by chaining him to a rock where his liver was destroyed by an eagle every day then made whole again each night throughout eternity.

5. William Shakespeare, *Hamlet*, ed. Barbara Mowat and Paul Werstine, New York: Simon & Schuster Paperbacks, 1992, 5. 2. 395.

6. Adam Donaldson Powell, "Contemporary World Haiku." *The Poetic Achievement of Ban'ya Natsuishi,* ed. Santosh Kumar, India: Cyber.wit, 2009.

The Importance of Ban'ya Natsuishi

Santosh Kumar

P.B. Shelley aptly remarks: "Poetry is ever accompanied with pleasure: all spirits on which it falls open themselves to receive the wisdom which is mingled with its delight. A poet is a nightingale, who sits in darkness and sings to cheer its own solitude with sweet sounds; his auditors are as men entranced by the melody of an unseen musician, who feel that they are moved and softened, yet know not whence or why." This critical observation is fully applicable to the haiku poems of Ban'ya. No doubt, for an impressive lucidity and transparency of style combined with profound feelings the haiku of Ban'ya are unsurpassed in the contemporary world poetry.

It is necessary to know T.S. Eliot's views about poetry. He says that a great poet should avoid 'provinciality' and refrain from revealing any sort of one-sided extreme view. Moreover, it is imperative for the poets to be inspired by their tradition and classical writers. "His significance, his appreciation is the appreciation of his relation to the dead poets and artists. You cannot value him alone; you must set him, for contrast and comparison, among the dead (T. S. Eliot)." What, then, accounts for Ban'ya's great achievement as a poet, it might be asked after reading T. S. Eliot's apt observation?

Like Basho, Ban'ya too has extensively traveled across the globe in quest of new themes to derive strong nourishment and inspiration from diverse cultures. Natsuishi's numberless visits to several countries are the means by which he has made haiku poetry popular all over the world. This characteristic of Ban'ya reminds us of Basho. "Basho traveled to explore the present, the contemporary world, to meet new poets, and to compose linked verse together. Equally important, travel was a means of entering into the past, of meeting the spirits of the dead, of experiencing what his poetic and spiritual predecessors had experienced. In other words, there were two key axes: one horizontal, the present, the comtemporary world; and the other vertical, leading back into the past, to history, to other poems" (Haruo Shirane).

No doubt, the impressionistic and concise style of Basho's haiku had a great impact on Ezra Pound, Imagist poets and Ban'ya. Ban'ya's haiku have been composed in an impressive style full of conciseness, brevity and reflective tone. Ban'ya avoids metaphor and similes to discard any ornamental phrase for the sake of brevity.

The following haiku about the death of his parents reveal lyrical intensity at its best. Swinburne made a very apt critical observation about P. B. Shelley: "He was a at once the perfect singing god; his thoughts ,words and deeds all sang together." This is quite true and applicable about Ban'ya's haiku poetry:

News of my mother's death:
stirring muddy water
so cold

Coldness
of returning to my hometown
father and mother gone

My deceased father's shoes
fall apart
before my mother's corpse

The above haiku have an intense undercurrent of pathos showing overwhelming melancholy due to the sadder aspects of life. These haiku are quite poignant, and the intensity of emotion reaches its climax in the third haiku. No doubt, Ban'ya's moods, whether happy or sad, reveal his exquisitely mobile imagination.

Ban'ya innovation into haiku poetry popularized it forever. The following haiku leaves no doubt in our minds that Ban'ya has a real and vital knowledge of the human heart:

An endless helix
Sings silently
Inside our body

This haiku makes it evident that Ban'ya always strikes the readers with surprise and pleasure.

He has also composed several philosophical haiku. For example, we are quite attracted by this haiku:

The naked Buddha
Always surrounded
By the rich colors of nothing

The haiku reveal a shrewd insight into the Buddhist emptiness, void or nothingness. In a few words, Ban'ya wih consummate skill has revealed the essence of Buddhism.

No doubt, Ban'ya's haiku poetry shows a vast canvas and diversity. There breathes an atmosphere of mysticism in this haiku:

Walking is philosophy's
Best friend—
Voices from the clouds

A peculiar union of emotion and mysticism very aptly colors the haiku. At its best, Ban'y's haiku have a supreme literary value due to his plain and matter-of-fact style

Without a pillow I live
Within a tent
Blown by a strong wind

Sparkle, tiles!
To be trod on!
A fragrant wind

The above haiku clearly show an impressive lucidity and the perfection of well-bred ease in Ban'ya's style of writing haiku.

Further, it is quite significant to point out that Ban'ya is quite sensitive about the tragic potentialities of nuclear power plants.

Sixty-six years after Japan's defeat
white smoke
from a nuclear reactor

The above haiku aptly reveals the poet's deep concern about the vastly multiplied nuclear arsenal in the modern world. He wrote this haiku for the sake of life, in order to reach out through the brutal facts of the radioactive material to fundamental aspects of world peace so that we may avoid unparalleled catastrophe.

Ban'ya's haiku poems are full of grace and classic charm. His visionary trances in several haiku reveal how he confronts the internal and external realities of life. The artless art of a great haiku lies wholly in the workmanship. And in the style of writing innovative haiku, Ban'ya is one of the greatest haiku poets. Dryden (1631-1700) pointed out: "There may be too great a likeness, as the most skilful painters affirm, that there may be too near a resemblance in a picture; to take every lineament and feature, is not to make an excellent piece; but to heighten the beauties of some part, and hide the deformities of the rest...the employment of a poet is like that of a curious gunsmith, or watchmaker; the iron or silver is not his own, but they are the least part of that which gives the value; the price lies wholly in the workmanship."

This wise observation by one of the greatest English critics proves that a wise use of 'workmanship' and 'literary carpentary' is indispensable for writing great poems. This is quite true about Ban'ya' haiku displaying inventive language, which is the most necessary quality required to create great poetry. Ezra Pound had recognized the significance of new inventive style and forms:

> It was you who broke the new wood.
> Now is a time for carving.

Another significant fact is that all great haiku reveal a universal truth that strikes the chord in the heart of readers. This is quite evident while perusing Ban'ya's haiku poetry. There is no doubt that Ban'ya's haiku attract the readers due to his intensity and depth of feeling. The most characteristic quality of these haiku is the poet's full-throated ease and natural gift of evoking the subtle sense of mystery.

Moreover, an impressive brevity of style and an apt selection of words make Ban'ya unsurpassed in the art of writing haiku. These haiku reveal spontaneity and subtle simplicity of style, which leaves no doubt in our mind about his fresh originality, true inspiration. The imaginative fervor and impressive imagery of his haiku provide both pleasure and wisdom to all readers. This is quite evident in the following haiku:

In a sandstorm
my head is blown
into innumerable slopes

Lightning
Composing a haiku-
Grass pillow

His haiku reveal spontaneous style devoid of self-conscious art. We often notice in his haiku lyrical moments of remarkable sweetness. He always writes in a natural style discarding labored vocabulary:

Wall of mud-
electricity plunges a village
into insomnia

Solitude of the god
in the deep sea
of books

In several haiku Ban'ya throws off the mask of anonymity and reflects on "ruins of ancient Japan" and "a hundred versions of myself":

Left behind
in a hundred dreams
a hundred versions of myself

In the window a stranger-
under the floor
ruins of ancient Japan

The quality of his poetic genius is quite apparent in the above haiku that stimulate our imagination. The essential point is that in Ban'ya's haiku there is no laborious artistry. He himself declares in one of his haiku that his 'will and testament' is to write in 'transparent and lucid style'.

In addition to the above qualities of Ban'ya' poetry, it should be noted that his haiku are composed in the language of common people, and this fact compels our admiration, because instead of employing the conventional poetic style Ban'ya writes his haiku in the language of common speech devoid of any kind of gaudy, ornamental and artificial phraseology.

Another significant fact is that all great haiku reveal a universal truth that strikes the chord in the heart of readers. This is quite evident while perusing Ban'ya's haiku poetry. There is no doubt that Ban'ya's haiku attract the readers due to his intensity and depth of feeling. The most characteristic quality of these haiku is the poet's full-throated ease and natural gift of evoking the subtle sense of mystery.

It is quite right to point out that Ban'ya's haiku poetry doesn't necessarily follow the classic 5-7-5 pattern; it reaches deeper discarding monotonous ideas and vague fancies. The fact is that a haiku poet should refrain from rigidly and strictly following the classic 17 syllables pattern and using season words. What is more important is to compose haiku spontaneously and with full-throated ease. Ban'ya is quite successful in spontaneously composing extraordinary compositions showing the bitter truth and postmodern realities of the new millennium. The world-renowned Sayumi Kamakura, one of the greatest contemporary haiku poets, holding the same opinion, very aptly and judiciously remarks: "When I first began writing haiku, I was taught that a haiku poem had to contain season words. To be quite blunt, a poem was considered a haiku only if it contained season words. Should this criterion really hold? Season words are still merely words. As long as they are words, then the emotions the author attempts to convey with them should take precedence over the words themselves. The Japanese haiku that has touched me are those where the author's true sentiments burst from the words. What is most important in haiku is how much true feeling is included in the poem."

Enjoying Ban'ya Natsuishi's Haiku
Sayumi Kamakura

English translation by Leanne OGASAWARA

Ban'ya Natsuishi's international haiku journal **Ginyu** is published four times a year in Japan. I serve as an editor on the journal, which in addition to publishing many new and noteworthy haiku poems also contains articles on literary criticism, book reviews, and information about Ban'ya's activities and those of the journals's many friends. The journal also contains essays, including a series I write called, *Tenchi no hyojo* (Expressions of Heaven and Earth).

In the series, I usually pick up a keyword and explore the various ways this keyword is expressed in haiku. For example, examining such themes as "sea," "sky" or "trees," I utilize five or six poems to see how such themes are given expression and voice. These essays of mine will often include poems by Ban'ya Natsuishi, such as the following, which I discuss below.

階段を突き落とされて虹となる   『猟常記』（1983年）

Shoved off the stairs —
falling I become
a rainbow
Trans. Jim Kacian
From *The Diary of Everyday Hunting* (1983) 0

One usually doesn't use the expression "shoved down" when it is just one or two steps. And, of course, "shoved off" is quite different in meaning from simply "falling down" stairs. The hatred and malice is quite vivid in the poem, and reading we know that we are speaking of an act of murder. Why did the person commit such an act? Why did someone receive such ill intent? Perhaps the reason is hidden in the expression, "I become a rainbow."

Jesus Christ was crucified. Galileo Galilei was accused and killed by the Inquisition. The Jewish people were persecuted during World War II. Indeed, no matter what time and what place, we find human jealousy and fear; hatred and resentment and human beings engaged in extreme cruelty to other human beings, who in turn try to protect themselves. But is their death simply all there is to it? Does the person shoved down the stairs cease totally to matter? We know from history that the truth does appear sometimes after death and crimes and punishments reevaluated. Examples of regained honor are too numerous to mention. Even if the person is dead, the truth can still someday come out and shine brilliantly. In changing the murdered person into a rainbow, Ban'ya has restored the honor and glory of the woman and brought the truth into the light of day.

In the ancient past, rainbows were seen as a bridge between the gods and human beings. In the Bible, after the flood, the rainbow was taken as evidence of God's covenant with Noah. In Japan, rainbows are seen a pathways leading to the gods. Viewed as objects of awe, rainbows were also seen as sacred snakes. Our world is filled with those things that surpass rational thought, and rainbows, as objects of hope and salvation, are one of these things.

天ハ固体ナリ山頂ノ蟻ノ全滅　　　　　　　　『真空律』　（1989年）

The solidity of heaven—
0at the mountaintop
all the ants destroyed
Trans. Jim Kacian
From *Rhythm of Vacuum* (1989)

Until I read this haiku, I had always believed that heaven was a kind of realm composed of colorless, odorless and transparent gas. While

I thought there could be it might be a liquid quality, like the feeling of rains, I never imagined it would have any solid quality, such as the way a rock feels when held in the palm of one's hand. This poem moreover is intriguing in the way it utilizes the auxiliary verb "will become."

What would happen if the heavens above became solid like a rock? In the poem above, the ants crawling on the summit of the mountain— that very place closest to heaven—are annihilated. Usually, one doesn't pay so much attention to ants. However, imagining the plight of dozens or hundreds or even thousands all wiped out on the mountaintop is a startlingly depressing image, don't you think?

In Japanese mythology, when the sun goddess, Amaterasu, was hiding in the Celestial Rock Cave, the earth grew dark and was wrapped in unfathomable darkness. This caused even all the ants to die. The world only came back to life with the dancing of Ame-no-Uzume-no-mikoto. As all the other gods laughed at her dancing, Amaterasu growing curious as to what the fuss was all about emerged from her cave, bringing light back into the world again. When the heavens grew solid, it was not just that the ants had died. All the people died as well, and such was the extent of the annihilation that after all was said and done, even the ants were shown to have died as well. Nothing escaped the annihilation. Heaven is not always sparkling and full of tranquility. Nature can be severe and violent. Sometimes it can even be unforgiving to all life. It is something to be feared—and this intensity is highlighted in the poem by the use of the katakana script.

地の果ての光の網よみどりごよ　　　　　　　『楽浪』（1992年）

A net of light
at the end of the land!
A newborn!
Trans. Jim Kacian
From *Waves of Joy* (1992)

One of my favorite painters is the Italian Renaissance artist Raphael (1483 - 1520). The newborn in Ban'ya's haiku reminds me of a "Madonna and Child" by Raphael. With its restless eyes, soft cheeks and plump arms and legs, I imagine Ban'ya's newborn to be like this: a mischievous and precious little cupid. Like the young Christ baby, I image it to be perched on his mother Mary's knees—seemingly ready to jump up in play at any moment.

The "net of light" in the poem also calls to mind Jabob's Ladder. One imagines countless rays of light radiating through the clouds. The poem's ending, by using the Japanese ending-particle "yo," conveys a deep sense of love that seems to connect this all-encompassing light to that of the existence of the newborn. No one knows where the end of the earth lies. Even if one were to search for the rest of their life, it is not likely they would find a net of light rays where there they would discover a newborn child. This is, I think, the light of the future, which the poet wished to see for his own son; that is, it is a parent's great wish for their child: that they will always be healthy as if embraced in a beautiful net of life. One cannot help but feel moved by this honest prayer.

In my essay series, I used the "stairs" haiku for an essay on "rainbows" and the "solidity of heaven" haiku for an essay on "heaven." Likewise, the "net of light" haiku was used for an essay on "light." For those reading my columns they will already understand that my essays are not aimed at explaining the various poems. Although one can indeed get a feeling of the haiku through my essays, the essays are largely written out of pure inspiration inspired by the keywords—not the haiku per se. The real aim of my essays is to try and tease out the way reading haiku can be enjoyable. When people tell me, "reading haiku is fun," I am filled with great delight, because it's true!

「私は水」あらゆる塵を浮かべます　　『右目の白夜』（2006年）

"I'm water"
letting float on me
any dust
Trans. Jim Kacian
From *Right Eye in Twilight* (2006)

Whether a river, a waterfall, a lake, a swamp, a pond or in a puddle or rice field, dust floats on water. It even floats in beautiful clear streams, where perhaps it doesn't collect, but it does float along with the current. Where dust does collect, it can become a place to play. Leaves, twigs, and straw; and if light enough even sand and dirt will instantaneously float. What is more beautiful and evokes more serenity than the vision of cherry blossom petals floating along the river? It's like a prayer. Even these petals will break down over time and become dust. One could also try thinking of the dust from the water's point of view. What does water think of dust? Does the water wish dust would go away? Or does water actually like the dust floating within its embrace?

The above haiku, after all, begins with the phrase, "I'm water." The poem does not come down decisively in either way. The dust is not seen as good or bad; nor is it seen as beautiful or ugly. What is maybe wonderful is the way nothing that comes is resisted. Indeed, "any dust" is all and everything that is floating together down the water. There is no hesitation or stance—just a confidence in water's unflappability. The great breadth of heart and depth and richness of water is fully conveyed so that one cannot help but feel that all dust must truly float in joy.

月光を堪え忍ぶ山ここへ来い　　『神々のフーガ』（1990年）

Come here!
The mountain
enduring the moonlight!
Trans. Jim Kacian
From *The Fugue of Gods* (1990)

How beautiful the mountain is! How majestic it looms before us. It makes us feel so alive! When gazing at the mountain, one's heart opens and takes flight. Painful and negative thoughts disappear for a time. But why is moonlight something to be endured for the mountain? Bathed in moonlight in the middle of the night, the mountain becomes a dark silhouette, and we feel its height and its presence. It seems somehow inconceivable that the mountain would feel being lit up in the moonlight something to be endured.

Why is it suffocating at night? Why is the moonlight that thing which must be endured?

> Over the mountains,
> far to travel, people say,
> Happiness dwells.
> Alas, and I went,
> in the crowd of the others,
> and returned with a tear-stained face.
> Over the mountains,
> far to travel, people say,
> Happiness dwells.
> Trans: Jakob Kellner

The German poet, Karl Hermann Busse once wrote a poem called, "Over the Mountains." In the poem, we feel all of our longings to be held in the embrace of the mountains. Large and overflowing with majesty (maybe even like our parents), they tend to make us more hopeful of greater tolerance. Surely there are good things beyond the mountains. Surely we will encounter happiness and a better tomorrow there. No matter what mountain we are looking at; no matter whether success is already in the palm of one's hand or whether happiness is futile, somehow mountains inspire hope.

Isn't that how we feel when we look at mountains? Or am I wrong and only speaking of my own feelings? Perhaps the mountains are not there to grant human wishes and that this is why the mountains are sad.

A mountain like that would have to endure the moonlight. Ban'ya's poem seems to enter straight into the mountain's heart and in great sympathy, gently calls to the mountain, "Come here!"

I chose the haiku "I'm water" for an essay on "water." The haiku on "moonlight" was not selected for an essay on the moon, but rather on "mountains." Rather than working with literary concepts or principles, I tend to choose poems intuitively from my heart. Somehow certain poems are lodged in my mind and when a poem truly moves me, I find that I wish to write about the poem. This seems somehow important: to work with the poems in my writing. In other words, appreciating poetry is not simply about being moved. It is also about stopping to question whether there are not things about which the haiku is further appealing. One must quietly sit with poetry and intently look at it. In that way, one can really hear what the haiku is saying.

日本海に稲妻の尾が入れられる　　　　　『神々のフーガ』（1990年）

Into the Sea of Japan
the lightning's tail
is plunged
Trans. Jim Kacian
From *The Fugue of Gods* (1990)

A lightning storm is made known from its great flashes of light. Of course, there is also the sound of thunder to go along with the lightning. But in general, when we talk about lightning storms, we are thinking about those great dazzling flashes that light up the night sky, where we see intense and violent zigzag streaks of light traveling from the sky down to the ground. And, anything in lightning's path will be struck and burned—maybe even electrocuted. Lightning is indeed terrifying.

In the haiku above, we see the tail of the lightning plunging into the Sea of Japan. But wait? Usually, when lightning strikes the ground, it connects with its tip or end, right? In Ban'ya poem, however, the lightning seems to be traveling rotated at a 180 degree angle. What would happen in such a case? Well first of all, lightning grows a tail like an animal –or perhaps a gigantic creature with a head, like a snake or maybe a dragon. With its tail plunged into the sea, the entire length of its body would become exposed to our vision. Another point of interest is the mention of the Japan Sea. Looking on a map, we see that unlike the seemingly limitless waters of the Pacific Ocean, the Sea of Japan is quite hemmed in. Surrounded by Sakhalin Island, Russia, China and the Japanese archipelago, from above it must look almost like a great lake or swamp.

With its tail plunged into the Sea of Japan and its body elevated above the water, this lightning storm could only be a dragon or great snake. For the creature, the sea is not the sea, but more like a lake. Or perhaps not even a lake, the sea might be more like a pond or puddle to such a great creature. This is a haiku concerned with grand scales. But then this great creature moving to the dictates of its heart with flashes of terrifying light and roaring with thunder, is in fact just trying to play, like a kitten or puppy. It is a wonderful image don't you think?

朝日夕日も見えざる河口を母と呼ぶ　　　　　『猟常記』（1983年）

The estuary where
neither the rising sun nor the setting sun's visible
I call mother
Trans. Jim Kacian
From *The Diary of Everyday Hunting* (1983)

What kind of place is an estuary where neither the rising sun nor the setting sun can be seen? Where is such a place? An estuary sits facing the sea. Therefore, whether facing the north or facing the south, still somewhere along the infinite horizon one will catch a sight of the sun—either sunrise in the morning or sunset in the evening. The waters too would reflect the beautiful yellows and reds of these sunrises and sunsets. And the sky too. I become entranced just imagining it. But, in the estuary of this haiku, all of that is invisible. The estuary of the haiku is a place endlessly shrouded in darkness; an estuary closed off in hazy gray. And that is the place the poet calls "mother."

Is there such a place as this?

Taking "mother" as a hint, doesn't it perhaps suggest the uterus? Lying deep within the female body, the uterus is a place that does not know sunrises or sunsets. There, it is always dusk. For approximately 266 days, the unborn child grows in a mysterious state of chaos; always connected to the mother. The water of the estuary encounters that of the ocean, and without any effort, the waters are pushed out to merge with the great waters of the sea of life. I used the "Sea of Japan" haiku for an essay on "the sea." And I used the "estuary" haiku for one on "mother."

**

My essay series, *Tenchi no hyojo* has been included in **Ginyu** almost immediately from the journal's start, over fifteen years ago. During that time, I have examined many haiku, but I have probably taken up Ban'ya's haiku more than anyone else's. In writing my essays, what I have found most difficult is not straying fundamentally away from the poems. Trying to express those things I want to express, I do not remain strictly only on the haiku. But after all since these are my essays, it is up to me to decide how to handle this issue, and in the end I have come to feel that essays and haiku should be differentiated. That is, the essay should somehow inspire comparison to the original poems. But the essay shoul also be able to stand alone. This is, I believe, the key to the success of the *Tenchi no Hyojo* essays. Ban'ya's poems inspire so many associations. And, they allow the reader's imagination to take flight. This is the reason I have employed so many of his haiku. Or to put it another way, I would suggest that it is for the purpose of incorporating all these many elements into the work for which Ban'ya creates his haiku.

Review of Black Card by Ban'ya Natsuishi

Shirley Bolstok

Ban'ya Natsuishi, which is the penname of Masayuki Inui, was born in Aioi

City, Hyôgo Prefecture, Japan in 1955 is no stranger to Haiku. It seems to emanate from his soul. We are taken on a haunting Journey of which the "Black Card" comes in like a Dark Moon rising. The greeting card that is ironic, sarcastic, truthful, heartfelt but elusive like a butterfly we chase to understand. It is the Black Card we receive through an esoteric mail system that lets us know, the illusion is always present. "Our feeling have no right answer, the blue sky. This is a poetic trance that takes us through Ban'ya Natsuishi's perception of how life is viewed through life, death and handling catastrophic circumstances like a ballet of words that captures the moment even when the ballet dancer falls down to pick oneself up again to regain the dance.

He is attentive to nature that surrounds the darkness of our creations. I like how many variables of Haiku suits each and every stance of observance which varies away from the non- traditional to use of the traditional which makes a poignant statement in the description of what he experiences. He describes the death of members of his family such as his parents and grandparents. We are taken on a hike through his own reactions, perceptions, visuals and auditory reminders of the evolution of death versus life as "

on the crossroad of souls

watch and clock

must disappear

He wishes for a blissful sleep and a release of the pain

"Rainwater

Washing ashes of anger into the sea

My nap

I am intrigued with the reoccurrence of metaphors which Ban'ya Natsuishi refers to keep us navigated within his journey, such as constant references to fish which brings us to the Tsunami & the Nuclear Reactor as the realization of a cycle between life and death.

"Happiness

Fishy words

Flying in the sky

A Goldfish doing a headstand

in Summer is his

farewell posture

I throw down

a dead word

to a dead fish

Fish sleep while swimming

I'm weeping

While sleeping

The word black:

A parasol with Black roses

Opens on a bridge

It's a stage

The word Rain;
Torrential rain pours on
a word pursuing
a word

A chair is creaking
A crazy election
In a crazy season of rain

Constant back-ground noise in words like the broken robot who shouts "It's your fault", the voice of consciousness out of sync with our daily lives. The reference of a small ash while "families make merry while a wing of ash expanding in the sky which sits on your hair as a tiny God of Death smiling. This is a stark contrast of the light and dark side of life that brings us the "Black Card:

"The Grey line stretches
to the heart
from a black card

"This Autumn
It rains
Black Cards"

Ban'ya Natsuishi, speaks of radioactivity that mars the " Holy Ground" and I have found the book "Black Card" to be an ingenious work which takes us on a haunting journey through the eyes of the author. The only thing I recommend is to stay with every page of the book and do not start in the middle. He has many different memories, realizations, stark comments and visuals that jump around. Each connected through the Haiku which Ban'ya Natsuishi, demonstrates in to a perfect stance that brings you the "Dark Card" which has been sent to each of us. This is not a "feel good book", it is a book which is a look at grief. But is also a look at hope as we all wish for a dark dream to disappear with the sunrise.

Death is not the last answer
A bird singing
Behind the mountains

He states:

Haiku must be written
In rainbow language
The sea of Galilee

Ban'ya Natsuishi, has done just that!

Black Card: A Review
Usha Kishore

Black Card, a collection of 234 haiku is unique; it is exquisite, thought provoking and multifaceted. Usually, Japanese poetry is translated and presented as an English version; very often translation books present the text in the source language and the target language. This Haiku collection by Ban'ya Natsuishi (pseudonym of Masayuki Inui), published by Cyberwit, features the original Japanese text and its translation into English by the author and Eric Selland and into Spanish by Emilio Masiá. The audience for this anthology is wide: the Japanese reader, the English reader and the European and South American Spanish readers.

My review of this book, however, has its remits. While unable to comment on Japanese poetry or its Spanish translation, my review primarily looks at the English version auto –translated by Natsuishi and by Eric Selland. This review is not of a haiku expert, who would possibly examine the traditions and conventions of the verse form, but it is primarily based on the poetic and contextual elements.

Haiku as is popularly known is a traditional Japanese verse form with seventeen syllables and three lines (5,7,5). Historically Haiku can be traced back to 13th century Japan as the opening phrase of the *renga,* a syllabic oral poem which is generally 100 stanzas in length. Over the years, the form has evolved in Japan and spread to other parts of the world. *Black Card* borders on subversion, where the syllables have been routinely broken. Nevertheless, the philosophy of haiku has been maintained by the focus on a moment of time, the ability to create an enlightening moment in the reader and the presentation of images that are direct and intense. Natsuishi's collection with its brevity and power defines Ezra Pound's critique of the verse form: "The image itself is speech. The image is the word beyond formulated language."

The *Black Card*, as elaborated by Ban'ya himself, is "a crucial and final card given to a sportsman who violates the rules many times." Therefore, the title could be interpreted as the poet's satire of his own existential crisis, his disillusionment with the world or the general isolation of the poet as an intellectual being within society. The realities of the new world order and the poet's inner conflicts and his external environment are brilliantly compounded in the microcosm of the haiku.

A grey line stretches
to the heart
from a black card

This autumn
it rains
black cards

The thematic motif of death is recurrent throughout the collection. Death reincarnates in various forms in the various sections of the book. Death is a lyrical reflection, revealing tender moments of this solemn metaphysical theme:

A word
enters sleep
deathbed

Death is presented in concrete images, as a sketch of the phenomenon from a mortal perspective, interspersed with observations of nature, with an occasional mystical exploration:

Singing stars
over the gently sloping road
toward death

and

Cherry in bloom —
the task of stopping the breath
finished

The mourning of the family and the timeless human musings on death are portrayed in Natsuishi's poignant tercets, with their sensory images and minimalistic refrains:

Mournful loss!
A limitless slanted line:
a cherry petal

 and

Life is death,
death is life?
Sounds of leaking water

The mystical quality of death is highlighted in its eternal being and its traversing of temporal space. The language plays with the metaphysical quality of death, untying its mystery like a knot. Expression and comprehension are simultaneous here:

On the crossroad of souls
watch and clock
must disappear

The universal links of death to the stars is presented in the following lines. In sublime verse, the poet explores death across time and space and the music of stars:

Winds, human beings
and memories have vanished
sounds of stars

The effective use of pathetic fallacy in Natsuishi's haiku is striking, where the omnipresent Japanese 'Cherry blossom' even defines death in metaphysical terms.

Cherry in bloom —
the task of stopping the breath
finished

There are reflections on life after death and the summoning of the *Shinigami* or death spirit/god:

Death is not the last answer
a bird singing
behind the mountains

Sitting on your hair
a tiny god of death
smiling

Inevitably, death is followed by grief and mourning. It endows a sense of loss to the near and dear ones of the departed:

Coldness
of returning to my hometown
father and mother gone

Other thematic threads that run through the collection are culture, travel, environment, politics and art. The collection takes the reader on a tour of Japan and its landscape, through the streets of Tokyo on the wings of a dragon fly. The city of Tokyo and its feverish activities seem to surpass the *Shinto* gods:

A glass dragonfly
becomes a ball of fire
takes a tour of Tokyo

Far away from gods' breathing
I have a slight fever
in Tokyo

The evocation of cultural landscape is juxtaposed with an inscape of Natsuishi's mind as in the following haiku, where a Japanese garden and its elemental quality are evoked:

The wind
brushing away an old pond
is one of my haiku

The metanarrative and the act of writing hovers above what seems a Japanese painting or a zen garden:

Acrobatic clouds
above the pond, around it
a miracle of words

The cultural landscape is evoked through the legendary bamboo, a symbol of prosperity and the eternal Mount Fuji, a beloved motif of Japanese poetry.

Lovers lying
on bamboo sheaths
of gold leaf

Shadow Fuji, earthquake
and full moon
celebrate poets

Myths are a representation of any culture; they signify change and are disguised histories or allegories that can be re-interpreted and reinvented on a personal level. To a myth lover like me, the following Haiku was a dream. In Japanese myth, Izanami is the goddess of creation and death, who gave birth to the eight great islands of the

Japanese chain. She also gave birth to fire, which killed the goddess. The poet uses the myth to highlight his existential reflections on life and death, the eternal binary:

In the hollow of a horse-chestnut
the goddess Izanami
gave birth to fire

Using the metaphor of gods, Natsuishi exposes the traditionally monocultural Japanese mentality, awakening it to the plurality of the Shinto Gods:

Human singularity
pollutes
the plurality the gods

Another interesting mythical allusion is that of the monkey deity *Sarutahiko,* who is the God of Crossroads between heaven and earth. It is interesting to note that the monkey is part of the Eastern zodiac and is a tangible metaphor for change:

This mask:
an entrance
into monkey's next world

Japan's Buddhist heritage is highlighted in the following haiku. To the poet, Buddha is a household deity, a manifestation of nature and eternal consciousness:

Covered in obscure layers of dust
I'm polishing
the family Buddhist altar

Pine forest:
a smile remains
after Buddha's disappearance

Another element of Japanese culture in *Black Card* is the allusion to the legendary artist Katsushika Hokusai, whose *ukiyo-e* woodblock prints of illustrations in a triangle and other geometrical shapes are widely acclaimed and have influenced many Western artists including Claude Monet and Edgar Degas.

Imprisoned wisdom
seeing through
Hokusai's triangle

The experimentation with haiku as a travelogue is a novel one. Natsuishi paints the world in his haiku, as in a snapshot. The view of the Hungarian city of Pecs is defined from the skies thus:

Mirage after mirage
of white clouds
Pecs is a flower

The poet traverses continents with his verse from West to East from Seoul to Spain:

To rainy Seoul
I bring silence
and a poem

Rainy Medellin
the 2nd floor
a thundercloud of poets

I was particularly fascinated by the haiku on Israel, depicting its current political, religious and cultural tensions:

My bare feet
in Israel
without any trace of Jesus

Haiku must be written
in rainbow language
the Sea of Galilee

No fish from clouds
on the table
of Jesus

Watch again
Jesus's despair
made of rocks

The historicisation of Japan's links with the world is another novel theme that Natsuishi attempts. The Nigerian diplomatic and business links that work together to facilitate electricity transmission in Nigeria with Japanese technology constitute the section, "Nigerian Electricity":

A Japanese steel pillar
and a Nigerian concrete pillar
just married

They kneel in prayer
before electricity, gods
and the governor

The reader is reminded of Japan's long history of earthquakes. The earthquakes bring a sense of personal loss and reflection rather than an elucidation of seismic activity.   The Japanese stoicism on earthquakes and their acceptance of the Pacific "Ring of Fire" is marvellously portrayed:

An earthquake
shakes up a New Year's Day
of double mourning

Year of the great earthquake
ends
with warmth from my socks

Natsuishi's environmental awareness emerges as he raises his voice against nuclear reactors and historicises the Fukushima Daiichi Nuclear disaster of 2011, which followed an earthquake and tsunami:

Fukushima fire
bares its fangs
water weeping

The poet relives the nuclear bombing of Hiroshima and Nagasaki and questions the need for nuclear plants:

Sixty-six years after Japan's defeat
white smoke
from a nuclear reactor

The disaster is described in graphic and poignant terms in the minimalistic verse that is haiku. The analogy of the nuclear reactor to an ogre is striking:

Windy streets
cedar pollen and radioactivity
flying over them

Raw milk
poured on fields
nuclear reactor smoke

There is an ogre
named nuclear reactor
and friends, too

It rains
on brands
named Hiroshima and Fukushima

Nuclear reactors
on the island of earthquakes and tsunamis
cherry blossoms in full bloom

As mentioned in the opening paragraphs of this review, I am not competent enough to comment on the intricacies of haiku. Nevertheless, I can certainly say that the poet has stretched the form beyond its boundaries, beyond the borders of Japan to reach out to the wider world, creating a surprise with each new haiku in the collection, forcing the reader to think out of the form and seek alternative interpretations.

When any book of translation is reviewed, the translator is usually forgotten. As a translator, I would like to elaborate on the role of the translator/interpreter. Travelling between cultures and languages, a translator interprets the source text to the readers of the target language. The English translation by Natsuishi and Selland has truly conveyed the haikuist's exquisite craftsmanship to an occasional haiku poet like me. I am truly fascinated by the thematic threads in the collection. The translation has opened new doors to a culture that India and in fact, the rest of the world know little of, a culture filled with myth, tradition and folklore. The translation conveys that Natsuishi, like Hokusai, is impatient with the demands of the conventional verse form and moves away from the centre, indulging in new themes and motifs. It is obvious that Natsuishi is a master of his craft, well versed in haiku, not only by his knowledge and study of the verse form, but also his experiments with the form, its structure, meaning and thematic strains. Natsuishi is an exponent of haiku, both as a verse form and as a medium of expression. He has established it as a new eclectic form and taken it to the international stage; the English translation faithfully conveys the poet's craft to the world.

References

https://www.poets.org/poetsorg/text/haiku-poetic-form

https://ericselland.wordpress.com/2010/06/03/introducing-haikuist-natsuishi-banya/

CONTRIBUTORS

Adam Donaldson Powell (Norway) is a multilingual author, literary critic, and art photography critic; and a professional visual artist. He has published several literary books (including collections of poetry, short stories, and novellas, two science fiction novels, and essays) in the USA, Norway and India; as well as numerous works in international literary publications on several continents. He writes in English, Spanish, French and Norwegian. He has previously authored theatrical works performed onstage, and he has read his poetry at venues in New York City (USA), Oslo (Norway), Buenos Aires (Argentina), and Kathmandu (Nepal). His book "Gaytude" (co-authored with Albert Russo) won the 2009 National Indie Excellence Award in the category gay/lesbian non-fiction. Powell was also the winner of the Azsacra International Poetry Award in 2008, and the recipient of a Norwegian Foreign Ministry travel stipend for authors in 2005. Powell also took initiative to planning and organizing the "Words - one path to peace and understanding" international literary festival in Oslo, Norway in 2008. He has been an author under the Cyberwit label since 2005, and he has published 12 literary books since 1987.

Aiswarya T Anish is from Kerala, India. Her first poetry collection is 'The Crescent Smile' (2011).

Amitabh Mitra is a visual artist, poet and a medical doctor based in East London, South Africa. He heads the Department of Emergency Medicine at Cecilia Makiwane Hospital, Mdantsane, Eastern Cape.

Anna Cates resides in Wilmington, Ohio with her two cats, Freddie and Christine. She earned her M.A. in English and Ph.D. in Curriculum & Instruction/English from Indiana State University and her M.F.A. in Creative Writing from National University. She teaches English and education online for several universities and regularly contributes to literary publications.

Kalyan Panja is from Assam, India.

Malini is the Author of bestseller Flotsam of the Mind a collection of her poems, a journey into self as she calls it. She started her career as a Radio Jockey with All India Radio and went on to become a journalist. She worked with Zee News and CNN (cnnindia.com and e-biz Asia Program) before moving to the corporate world where she launched several new brands in the Indian market. After two decades she found her calling as an Artist. She is an Author, Painter and Photographer other than being an active Feminist residing in Singapore.

Marta Knobloch has written five collections of poetry, four of them award winning: The Song of What Was Lost, The Mayor and City Council of Baltimore, 1988 (Artscape Literary Arts Award of Baltimore); Sky Pond, Washington, D.C.: S.C.O.P. Publications, 1993 (Co-winner of the Columbia Book Award); and The Room of Months / La stanza dei mesi, Bologna, Italy: Book Editore, 1995 (Lions Ferrara Castello's Premio Donna); Cloud Compass: New and Selected Poems, Honorable Mention for Writer's Digest's Self-Published e-Book Awards in the Poetry category, 2015. Her ecological fable, How Djambawa Found What He Was Seeking, was published in Italian in Ferrara, Italy, and awarded the Premio di Arte e Ambiente di Italia in 1991. Her work has appeared in numerous literary magazines and anthologies in the United States, Australia, Ireland, Italy and England. She has traveled extensively throughout her life, lived abroad, and now makes her home in El Paso, Texas. To learn more about her work, visit her website at www.martaknobloch.com.

Santosh Kumar (b. 1946) is a poet, short-story writer and an editor from UP India; DPhil in English; Editor of *Taj Mahal Review* and *Harvests of New Millennium* Journals; several awards; member of World Poets Society (W.P.S.); member of World Haiku Association, Japan; presented papers in the seminar, interviews as special guest at international literary festival WORDS – one path to peace and understanding Oslo, Norway in September 2008; attended 20th Annual International Literary Festival *Druskininkai Poetic Fall* and 5th World Haiku Association Conference in Lithuania, Sept 30 to Oct 5, 2009; published poetry in *Indian Verse by Young Poets (1980), World Poetry* (1995 & 1996), *The Fabric of A Vision* (2001), *The Still Horizon* (2002), *The Golden Wings* (2002), *Voyages* (2003), *Symphonies* (2003), *New Pegasus* (2004), *Explorers* (2004), *Dwan* (USA), *Promise (Purple Rose Publications, USA), World Haiku 2008 No. 4, World Haiku 2009 No. 5, Taj Mahal Review (2002, 2003, 2004, 2005, 2006, 2007 & 2008).* He has also edited sixteen World Poetry Anthologies, and four books of World's Great Short Stories. He is also the author of a collection of poems entitled *Helicon* (Cyberwit, India, ISBN 81-901366-8-2), Haiku collection *New Utopia* (Rochak Publishing, India ISBN 978-81-903812-0-8), *NO NUKES: Brave New World of Beauty, A Long Narrative Poem, Songs of Peace & Haiku* (Rochak Publishing, India ISBN 978-81-903812-3-9), and *Critical Essays* in collaboration with Adam Donaldson Powell (Cyberwit, India, 978-81-8253-110-9). He has also edited *The Poetic Achievement of Ban'ya Natsuishi* (Cyberwit, India, ISBN: 978-81-8253-149-9). His another book of literary criticism is entitled *Adam Donaldson Powell: the Making of a Poet* (Cyberwit, India, ISBN: 978-81-8253-163-5). His other books include The Haiku of *Sayumi Kamakura: A Critical Study*, and *Haiku of the Present.*

Sayumi Kamakura She was born in Japan, 1953. Began composing haiku in her twenties. In 1998 she established the haiku magazine *"Ginyu"* with Ban'ya Natsuishi, and has been its Editor. Has attended haiku or poetry festivals held in Japan, Slovenia, Portugal, Bulgaria, inner Mongolia, Estonia, Lithuania, Hungary and India. She won the Oki sango Prize in 1988, the Modern Haiku Association Prize in 2001, AZsacra International Poetry award for Taj Mahal Review in December 2012 Issue. Her haiku collections include: *Jun* (*Moisture*, 1984), *Kamakura Sayumi Kushu* (*Haiku of Sayumi Kamakura*, 1998),

Hashireba haru (Run to Spring, 2001), umi wa la la la(La la la the sea, 2011).She co-authored *Gendai Haiku Panorama* (1994), *Gendai Haiku Shusei Zen 1 Kan (Contemporary Haiku Anthology in One Volume,* 1996), etc. Published in both Japanese and English are *A Singing Blue* (2000) and *A Crown of Roses* (2007). Published in Romanian are *Stolen by the moonlight*(2012), etc. Her haiku has been translated into English, Greek, Russian, Bulgarian, Portuguese, Korean, Mongolian, Romanian, Serbian, Estonian, Lithuanian, Hungarian, etc. She is the Treasurer of the World Haiku Association. Judge of the Haiku section of Japanese daily newspaper of The Asahi Shimbun's Saitama culture.

Shirley Bolstok was born and raised in Denver, Colorado. "My parents are Holocaust Survivors. Writing has always been an integral part of my life. I like writing about the shifting of our existence, whether it is ethereal, emotional or physical. I have had many publications of my work including poetry, haiku and quotes in newspapers, anthologies, books and online magazines. I now have three books published, Impassioned Soul, a volume of poetry, Apples From the Tree of Life and Grapes From the Vines of Life. Growing up as a child of Survivors of the Holocaust has given me a very different perspective of humanity from an early age. I have many contrasting views of the windows of life. Each has its own dimension and density. I have a diverse background and education and have appreciated the variety of insights that it has brought me. Time and consciousness are always in motion. We are powerful beings with the ability to create straight from the heart of God.

Usha Kishore: Indian born Usha Kishore is a poet, editor and translator from the Sanskrit, resident on the Isle of Man, where she teaches English at Queen Elizabeth II High School. Kishore is internationally published and anthologised by *Macmillan, HodderWayland, Oxford University Press* (all UK) and *Harper Collins India* among others. Her poetry has won prizes in UK Poetry competitions, has been part of international projects and features in the British Primary and Indian Middle School and Undergraduate syllabi. The winner of an Arts Council Award and a *Culture Vannin* Award, Kishore's debut collection *On Manannan's*

Isle was published in 2014 by *dpdotcom,* UK. A second collection, *Night Sky between the Stars* (*Cyberwit,* India) and a book of translation from the Sanskrit, *Translations of the Divine Woman,* from (*Rasala,* India) have been published in 2015. Usha was recently conferred with the *Word Masala* Lifetime Achievement in Poetry Award at the House of Lords, UK. A third poetry collection is forthcoming in 2017 from *Eyewear Publishing,* London. www.ushakishore.co.uk